AUTOMATIC WEALTH for GRADS

...and Anyone Else Just Starting Out

MICHAEL MASTERSON

Foreword by Mark Skousen

John Wiley & Sons, Inc.

For Liam, Patrick, and Michael.

Published by John Wiley & Sons, Inc., Hoboken, New Jersey.
Published simultaneously in Canada.

For general information about our other products and services, please contact our Customer Care Department within the United States at 800-762-2974, outside the United States at 317-572-3993 or fax 317-572-4002.

Wiley also publishes its books in a variety of electronic formats. Some content that appears in print may not be available in electronic books. For more information about Wiley products, visit our web site at www.wiley.com.

Library of Congress Cataloging-in-Publication Data

Masterson, Michael.
    Automatic wealth for grads—and anyone else just starting out /
Michael Masterson
      p. cm.
   ISBN-13: 978-0-471-78676-4 (cloth)
   ISBN-10: 0-471-78676-4 (cloth)
    1. College graduates—Finance, Personal. 2. Youth—Finance,
Personal. 3. Saving and investment—United States. 4. College
graduates—Employment—United States. 5. Vocational
Guidance—United States. I. Title.
  HG179.M315 2006
  332.024'01—dc22

2005032768

Printed in the United States of America

10 9 8 7 6 5 4 3 2 1

CONTENTS

ACKNOWLEDGMENTS

My first debt of gratitude goes to Michael Ward, who suggested the title after *Automatic Wealth* hit the best-seller lists. Next, I'd like to thank Judy Strauss, Charlie Byrne, Suzanne Richardson, Kim Twist, Maggie Crowell, Wayne Ellis, Debbie Englander, and Justin Ford for their help, wisdom, and encouragement.

And finally, the inspiration to finish this book was sustained by my love for my children, nieces, nephews, and godchildren who, I hope, will one day read and profit from it: Eamon, Morgan, Allison, Annabelle, Shay, Elizabeth, Christopher, Justin, Thadeus, Morgan, Vivian, Jocelyn, Isabelle, Conor, Aidan, Alexandra, Vincent, Emma, and Louis.

FOREWORD

In short, the way to wealth, if you desire it, is as plain as the way
to market. It depends chiefly on two words, *industry* and *frugality*;
that is, waste neither time nor money, but make the best use of
both. Without industry and frugality, nothing will do, and with
them everything.

—Ben Franklin, *The Way to Wealth*

This is a "how to" book for people who have the *drive* to be
eminently successful in life. Do you have what it takes?

A hundred years ago, aspiring young entrepreneurs like
Andrew Carnegie and Thomas Mellon learned their "way to
wealth" by reading Ben Franklin's *Autobiography*. Today's grads
might well learn the same tried-and-true principles from
Michael Masterson's *Automatic Wealth for Grads*.

There is an uncanny resemblance between the two sages.
Franklin tells his rags-to-riches story in the *Autobiography*,
emphasizing three grand principles:

1. *Industry and smart work:* As Franklin was starting out as
   a printer in Philadelphia, he worked harder, longer,
   and smarter than his competitors. He was the first to
   arrive at work in the morning and the last to leave. He
   made sure that his customers saw him carrying the
   newspapers himself through the streets of Philadelphia.
   He wanted the public to know he was an ambitious
   young man deserving of their business.

   Franklin opposed taking advantage of a neighbor or
   customer. He believed that every transaction should be
   an honest one that benefits both buyer and seller.

But working long hours can only get you so far. You have to develop business acumen. You need to train yourself in the most advanced techniques. You need to be ahead of your competition. Franklin invested in the latest printing equipment from Britain, while his competitors used old equipment. He developed close friendships with customers and suppliers through his Junto, a club of fellow tradesmen. Franklin was the only founding father who was approachable, the kind of guy you could sit down and have a beer with. He got involved in civil affairs to improve the city—paving the streets and starting the first library, university, fire station, and insurance company. He worked with government officials and got the contract to print the province's currency. Franklin was also a practical inventor—of a new, more efficient stove, lightning rods to prevent fire caused by lightning, bifocals, and a musical instrument.

Franklin used leverage. He opened up several franchises of his printing services in the other colonies and the Caribbean. When he retired at age 42, he had a large source of regular income from these franchises and other investments.

2. *Frugality and economy:* Franklin adopted the principles of budgeting, wise use of time, and avoiding waste throughout his long life. "Economy is a great source of revenue," he wrote in *Poor Richard's Almanac.* His most famous pro-saving adage, "A penny saved is a penny earned," is remarkably profound. How can a penny saved be a penny earned? Assume you earn $100 a day. If you have $100 in your pocket and you spend it, you have to go out and do a day's work to get that $100 back. Another way of putting it: With $100 in savings,

you could take off a whole day of work and still enjoy a day's income by drawing upon your savings. In sum, saving is a source of earning power.

The more you save, the more earning power you build up. In addition, savings earn interest, which means more earning power through compounded returns. Thrift is always a virtue, and debt is always a danger, for individuals, businesses, and nations.

Franklin preached economy in peacetime and wartime, when he was poor and when he was rich. He believed in modest living and avoiding extravagant lifestyles that might create envy among neighbors.

MICHAEL MASTERSON: A MODERN-DAY DR. FRANKLIN

I am glad to see my friend Michael Masterson following in the footsteps of the wise ol' Dr. Franklin. What does Mr. Masterson preach? First, he preaches thrift, and the power of compounded interest. After you pay your taxes, "pay yourself," he admonishes. Save at least 15 percent of your after-tax income. That's a tall order, especially for someone just starting out in business. But it can be done. John Templeton, the famed mutual fund guru, saved 5 percent of his income during the 1930s Great Depression. I know others today who save 35 percent of their income.

Second, he preaches economy and modest living, even when you are wealthy. He rejects the Keynesian mind-set of the consumer society; instead, he advocates the frugal society. Buy a used BMW, not a new one, and save. Don't buy an expensive, big house. "Buy the house you most admire, which is probably not huge and flashy," he says. "Less is more."

"Overspending is a major problem," he declares. He tells the story of Mike Tyson, who made more than $300 million during his boxing career, and went bankrupt. Franklin wisely said, "Revenue without economy is never sufficient." Masterson says the same thing. So does George Clason in his classic book *The Richest Man in Babylon*. To make sure to get richer every year, always spend less than you make. Always.

Most people think the way to wealth is by earning more money, by getting a raise, inheriting a fortune from a rich uncle, or winning the lottery. Actually, Masterson offers a lot of good advice for getting a raise or increasing your income dramatically, and it is sound advice. Read those chapters carefully. But just remember, making more money is no guarantee of financial success. You need to live within your means, and you need to protect your backside, and you need to keep a budget. Remember how John D. Rockefeller succeeded? He would tell you very simply: "Ledger A." He kept an accurate count of his revenues and expenditures.

Then there is the principle of sound investing. What good is it if you save 15 percent and foolishly invest it in scams and bad investments? Masterson shows you how to invest your surplus wealth prudently in the stock market, real estate, and other alternative investments. He has excellent chapters on investing your savings wisely, based on experience and the sound advice of experts. "Learn to earn," as Peter Lynch says. You'll make the mistakes, but you'll learn from those mistakes and do better.

I like Masterson's fundamental approach to stock market investment. Invest in growth, in companies that can't help but burgeon over time, and buy them cheaply, at a discount. J. Paul Getty said it best in his classic work, *How to Be Rich*: "Sound stocks, purchased for investment when their prices are low and held for the long pull, are very likely to produce high profits through dividends and increases in value." Masterson is a second-generation J. Paul Getty. He recommends the same practical advice to you. Buy small-cap stocks that are growing rapidly. (I would only add that you should consider investing abroad—foreign stocks often offer excellent profit potential.)

Finally, I'd like to compliment Mr. Masterson for his ethical approach to business and investing. He confesses that early in his career, he was more interested in making a buck than in his integrity. "In my early years as a marketer, I sold products I wasn't proud of at prices I couldn't justify." But he learned, as we all do eventually, that the right way of doing business is the best way. Dr. Franklin would find it most agreeable.

I especially enjoyed reading Chapter 9, the final chapter, "Living Rich Starting Tomorrow." This is a chapter that only a seasoned veteran could write: "Slow down to enjoy life. . . . Eliminate major time killers like television, video games, and Web browsing. . . . Reduce stress in your life by making time for your favorite pastimes. . . . Get a restful night's sleep. . . . Take regular work breaks. . . . Leave your work at work. . . . Stop thinking about yourself." You might do well to read another book along these lines: *The Importance of Living*, by Lin Yutang, the Chinese-American philosopher. "O wise humanity, terribly wise humanity! Of thee I sing. How inscrutable is the civilization where men toil and work and worry their hair gray to get a living and forget to play!"

Of course, Masterson says that "few people" really understand these sound principles, and so they struggle financially throughout their lives. Franklin said it well, "Experience keeps a dear school, yet fools will learn in no other." Hopefully, you are different because you have bought this book. Only time will tell whether you will have the guts and honor to follow Masterson's masterful plan. Good luck!

—*Mark Skousen*
February 2006

CHAPTER 1

———

WEALTH MATTERS: YOU DECIDE HOW MUCH

Making money is not the most important thing in life. And Getting rich shouldn't be your number one goal.

But as a recent college graduate (or young person embarking on a career), wealth building should be on your agenda. Because—like it or not—your financial situation will affect your ability to enjoy every other aspect in your life.

They say the three most important questions a young person must answer are:

1. What shall I do with my life?
2. Where shall I do it?
3. And with whom?

In answering those questions, it makes sense to consider your finances because they will determine the choices you have in developing a career, selecting a place to live, and taking care of yourself and your family.

This book is based on the wealth-building principles outlined in my best-selling book, *Automatic Wealth*. But the ideas presented here are tailored specifically to you. As a recent graduate (and young person starting out), you have an advantage that I don't have. It is an amazingly powerful advantage that makes it absolutely *easy* to get rich.

When you have 60 years of life ahead of you, becoming wealthy is not just easy, it can be automatic. And that's the purpose of this book: to give you a blueprint for automatic wealth.

Automatic Wealth. What does that mean?

You understand the meaning of *automatic:* having the ability to develop independently, that is, without conscious effort. The wealth-building skills that you will learn in this book are easy. If you start practicing them now (I'll show you how), then before you know it you will be doing them without conscious effort. At that stage you will be an automatic wealth maker.

That's what I mean by *automatic*. Now let's deal with the tougher word: *wealth*. What does it mean to be wealthy?

Your idea of what it means is probably different from mine. This point, though obvious, was underlined for me recently when we asked the 450,000 readers of my daily e-zine *Early to Rise* (EarlytoRise.com), to define wealth. Here are a few of the hundreds of answers we received:

- Having everything you want
- Having more than you need
- A million dollars in the bank
- Ten million dollars in savings
- Making a million bucks a year

- Making a hundred thousand dollars a year
- Living the life of a rock star

Even experts disagree on what it takes to be wealthy.

To Blanche Lark Christerson, director of the Wealth Planning Group at Deutsche Bank, wealthy is a net worth of $15 million. Christerson figures that for married couples with two young kids, today's "pricey lifestyle" costs about $275,000 a year. If you are single with no dependents, Christerson says $10 million will do. (She's assuming that you'd have 45 years ahead of you and that you'd want to preserve capital and leave it to your heirs or charities. She's calculating a conservative 3.5 percent return on investments.)

To certified financial planner Jon Duncan, it's a net worth of $7.5 million. Duncan is making the same assumptions as Christerson in terms of kids and life span, but he thinks it only takes about $200,000 a year to live rich. And because the stock market has historically yielded about 10 percent, he's figuring on your getting a much better return on your savings. (From Jeanne Sahadi, "How Rich Is Rich?", July 24, 2003, accessed at http://www.cnn.com September, 2005.)

Yes, wealth is a relative concept. But in order to talk about it productively, we must agree on a single definition. For the purposes of this book, then, I'm going to ask you to accept this one:

Wealth is a store of something valuable, something you can use or enjoy later. Financial wealth, therefore, is the net savings you have put aside for spending in the future.

Note the phrase "net savings." That means the money you have saved that doesn't need to be used for any current needs or any current debts. That is to say, your financial wealth is the amount of money you have put aside that is free and clear for future use.

Some financial experts (such as Christerson and Duncan) classify wealth as your net worth. Net worth is the total of all your financial assets minus all your debts. My definition—net savings—is a little more stringent. I'm not letting you count the financial value of your house, your car, or any other key possessions that you wouldn't be willing to get rid of someday.

The reason for this stricter definition is simple: You are always going to need a house and a car, so you can't really count them as part of your wealth. (This is an oversimplification. If you figure your wealth this way, you will be erring on the side of conservativeness. That's a good thing. It means you will always be richer than your numbers say you are.)

If you accept this definition—or even if you would rather count your wealth using the standard net worth formula—you must still recognize one important fact: You need more than a high income to be wealthy. It's amazing how many young people (and lots of older people) don't understand this. Too many folks equate making "mucho dinero" with being rich.

A good example: the cable TV show *Entourage*. In *Entourage*, the main character is a fictionalized version of Mark Wahlberg after he became famous as a Hollywood actor. Mark's character and his friends spend all their time and money buying toys and chasing girls, while their accountant sits in his office and screams at them. The entourage is hell-bent on spending every cent of the multimillion-dollar income their buddy is earning. And that makes them feel rich. The truth is, however, that they are just as broke as they were when they were living in Brooklyn. The only difference is that they are spending more.

To be rich, you need lots of money in the bank. A big

THE SAD STORY OF MIKE TYSON: A SPENDING FOOL

During the 20-year span of his career, Mike Tyson's income exceeded $400 million. Yet in 2004, before his thirty-ninth birthday, this amazing moneymaker was $38 million in debt. He had some assets—equity in some mansions, some cars, and some jewelry—but insiders speculate that their total value was less than $3 million. For the sake of wishing him well, let's assume it was twice that much. That would put his personal net worth at minus $32 million.

Think about that. Minus $32 million!

With a negative net worth that large, Mike Tyson is 150,000 times poorer than the average wage earner from Sierra Leone, the poorest country in the world, with an average annual income of $200 per person.

"How can a man with a $4 million estate in New Jersey be poor?" a colleague asked me.

"He can still make millions every time he fights," she said. "Anyone who can make millions isn't poor."

Yet by every recognized standard of accounting, he is poor. Extremely poor.

But he doesn't think so. And that's part of the reason he got so poor in the first place. The faster money came in, the faster it went out. Stories about his profligacy are already legendary. Tyson employed as many as 200 people, including bodyguards, chauffeurs, chefs, and gardeners.

He spent:

- Nearly $4.5 million on cars and motorcycles
- $3.4 million on clothes and jewelry
- $7.8 million on 'personal expenses"

(continues)

5

- $140,000 on two white Bengal tigers and $125,000 a year for their trainer
- $2 million on a bathtub for his first wife, actress Robin Givens
- $410,000 on a birthday party
- $230,000 on cell phones and pagers during a three-year period from 1995 to 1997

The purpose of this is not to shake a finger at Mike Tyson but to alert you to the dangerous temptation to spend more when you make more. As someone who grew up drinking powdered milk and wearing hand-me-downs, I understand the strength of that temptation.

income can give you a great lifestyle—but if you are spending it as fast as you are making it, when you stop working, or when a financial emergency arises, you'll very quickly find out how *un-rich* you really are.

Mike Tyson made more than $300 million during his boxing career. But today, he's in debt. Big debt. If Don King, his manager and promoter, had helped Mike learn to save his money (instead of spending it on $3 million rings), Mike would be wealthy. Instead, he's probably one of the poorest men on earth.

If you want to become wealthy—in terms of having lots of money put away for a rainy day . . . or money to spend after you stop working for it—then you are going to have to learn how to save and invest a significant portion of your income.

But here's the good news. You are young, so this is a *really good time* for you to start saving money. If you get yourself into the habit of doing so now, you'll be rich before you know it.

In Chapter 2, I'll tell you exactly why being young gives you such a great advantage when it comes to building wealth. I'll explain why every dollar you save is worth $5 or $10 more than every dollar your parents saved. You'll discover the true power of compound interest and find out how to make it work for you.

But let's get back to this idea of stored value, which—in financial terms—translates into savings.

The purpose of saving money is so that if and when you stop working, you can draw on your savings to pay for your living expenses. For many people, the ideal situation is to have enough money saved that they can live off the interest. If, for example, your lifestyle (including paying your debts) costs you $70,000 a year and you have a million dollars in savings generating 7 percent interest (or $70,000 in income), you are financially independent.

Another, rather crude, way of saying this is that you have "G.L." (Get Lost) money.

G.L. money. Isn't that a good objective? Wouldn't you like to have the ability to *not* work and yet pay for all your living expenses? Wouldn't it be great to spend your time focusing on the activities that give you the greatest satisfaction in life, without worrying about money?

That's exactly what I'm going to show you how to do: Create a plan to get you from where you are today to a state of financial independence—having G.L. money. (I'm assuming you are broke and saddled with student loans. If you are better off than that, my plan will work that much faster.)

Okay. So how do we figure out how much in savings is enough?

We have to start with how much income you think you

will need to live the life you want to live. To help you think about this, I'll tell you a little story about my early years—when I was just a few years older than you and knew even less about wealth and money than you probably do now.

IT'S NOT JUST ABOUT SAVINGS— YOUR INCOME MATTERS

As a young man, I never had any ambitions about making money. I knew nothing about business and didn't care to learn. My goal in life was to write a great novel, marry a beautiful woman (who liked my novel), and travel.

Apart from finishing that novel, I got what I wanted. And along the way, I also got rich. Here's what happened.

It was 1983. I had just been hired as editorial director for a fledgling newsletter-publishing company in South Florida. Because I had to give the occasional speech, I enrolled myself in a Dale Carnegie course on public speaking. Somehow, I ended up in the Carnegie basic success course instead.

How to Win Friends and Influence People is a 14-week program in which you are asked to focus on a certain character-changing task each week and then report on your progress the following week.

I was the worst student in the class. Cynical and suspicious, I despised what I took to be the silly, do-goodish prattle of the teachers. But I'd paid good money to be there, so I begrudgingly went along with the program—and I'm very glad I did.

The assignment for week four was to come up with a single goal that you would pursue for the remaining 10 weeks of the program. The idea was that by concentrating on only one goal, you could make much more progress than you would with a wider scope of objectives.

Sure enough, I had a hell of a time with that lesson. For me, it was by far the most difficult of the 14.

When I first started listing my goals, I could think of only two or three. But as I put more thought into it, the list began to expand . . . first to half a dozen . . . then to 10 . . . and then 20 . . . and on and on. Narrowing down the list was torture. Among other things, I wanted to be a great writer, a wise teacher, an admirable dad and husband, a linguist, a wine connoisseur, an athlete, and more. I was paralyzed. I simply couldn't tolerate the idea of giving up any one of those goals.

Finally, driving to the class at which I was to publicly announce my one main goal, I had a breakthrough. I realized that all my hard work and ambition had amounted to nothing, because I had been spreading myself too thin.

Then I had an idea: "Why not make 'making money' my number one goal?" I thought. "If I achieve that goal, I'll have all the money I need to pursue my other interests."

At the time, I knew nothing about making money. But I focused on that one goal and made it my priority. And it worked. Big-time.

Before that experience, I was making $35,000 a year. A year later, my yearly income was $150,000 a year. (Later on in this book, I'll tell you how you can boost your income that dramatically.) Needless to say, this was more money than I had ever imagined I'd make. So I wasn't quite sure how to feel about it.

"You should feel very good," Ron (my accountant at the time) told me. He was amused by my innocent excitement. Ron was used to working with high-income earners—most in the million-dollar-plus category. "Welcome to the world of the rich," he said.

"Come on," I said. "A hundred and fifty grand is nothing compared to what most of your clients make."

"It's time you learned something about money," he replied.

I perked up and listened. To this day, I've never forgotten what he said. "First of all, you have to recognize that as far as earning income is concerned, you are already in the top 5 percent. Second, you need to know that $150,000 is enough to live like a billionaire."

"How can you say that?" I asked.

"Think of it this way," he said. "When you have a family income of less than $50,000, it's a struggle."

"Tell me about it," I replied. "I have been struggling ever since I graduated from college."

"Then, when you boost your income to between $50,000 and $150,000, you have everything you need but you have only some of what you want."

Since my transition from below $50,000 to $150,000 had been so quick, I had never had the time to experience living at that level of income. So I asked him what he meant.

"I mean this. You can afford a nice, modern, modest home. And you can pay your bills. You can even go out to dinner at a good restaurant once a week and spend a few weeks a year vacationing. But you can't do any of those things too elaborately, and you can't afford to buy yourself toys."

"Toys? Such as?"

"Such as sports cars, boats, expensive watches, and so on."

"My $35 Casio watch is fine for me," I said. "And I get seasick. But I wouldn't mind a little red sports car."

"Well, guess what?" he said. "Now you can afford that, too."

"Do you really think so?"

"Sure. Buy yourself a little five-year-old convertible for $3,500." (Remember, this was 1983.) "Keep it in your garage. Take it out on weekends."

"I'd love that."

"Now that you are in the $150,000 club, you can have

everything you need and everything you want. You just have to be sure that you don't overspend on what you want."

"Like limiting the money I spend on my sports car to $3,500."

"Exactly. The only difference between your lifestyle and the way my wealthiest clients live—and I'm talking about guys who rake in eight-figure incomes every year—is the price of your toys. Other than that, you are living the same."

"That's a great thought," I told Ron. "Very comforting."

"And here's something else you need to know," he said, as he packed up his papers and started to walk out of the room. "You'll get just as much fun out of your $3,500 sports car as any of my other clients get from their Lamborghinis or Maseratis."

Do you know what? Ron was right. I bought a Triumph, a TR-6, for $3,200—it was the best sports car I ever owned.

That conversation with Ron left a deep impression on me. It was definitely a turning point in my financial life. Were it not for the advice he gave me, I might well have gone on to do what most high-income earners in America do: spend my money as fast as (or even faster than) I made it.

Overspending is a major problem for high-income earners for several reasons:

- They want to show off their income by purchasing status symbols.
- They want to reward themselves by buying expensive toys.
- They feel that as long as they can pay for what they buy, there isn't any problem. If they spend every dollar of what they make this year, there'll be plenty more dollars next year.

The trouble with this sort of thinking is obvious: It makes it very difficult for one to save. And if you don't save money, you can't get richer. Wealth is not about how much you make. It's about how much you have to spend in the future. Put in financial terms: Wealth is not your income, but your net savings.

Ron's conversation was immensely helpful to me, because he made me understand, at the beginning of my high-income-earning years, that spending extra money on ever-more-expensive toys wasn't going to give me any more gratification. All it was going to do was put me on the same treadmill with everyone else in my category (the rest of the 5 percent in the $150,000 club), most of whom would never end up wealthy.

So that's an important thing for you to recognize now, too: As you follow the steps laid out in this book and begin to earn a higher and higher income, don't fritter it all away by being lured into buying more expensive toys.

The first couch I bought cost $400. I remember thinking, "It doesn't get any better than this." And it never did. The couches I buy today give me no more pleasure, comfort, or space. Yet they cost much more.

What happened? Did I miss out on some inflationary spiral? The truth is that my own success victimized me. In earning more, I allowed myself to spend more on things like couches. If I had gotten more out of those things, that would have been fine. But I didn't.

Master wealth builders understand a secret that it took me years to learn: You have to keep your spending down while your income increases.

Let's take another look at the three levels of income that Ron identified—and how they can affect your lifestyle.

THE THREE LEVELS OF INCOME

1. If you have a family income of less than $50,000, it's tough to make ends meet.

WHY STRIVE FOR FINANCIAL FREEDOM?

The main purpose of this book is to help you become an automatic wealth builder so that—maybe before you know it—you will achieve financial independence.

Think about the term *financial independence*. What does that mean? And why should you want it? Here are some possibilities:

- You may want more freedom in your life—more choice about where you live, how you live, how much you work, and so on.
- You may want more leisure in your life. You don't want to feel compelled to work 8 or 10 hours every day, or five and six days every week.
- You may want more tranquility in your life—an end to the stress that lack of money sometimes causes. You want to be able to sleep easily at night and enjoy your days without worry.

Those goals are all reasonable, laudable, and possible. And they are all attainable if you'll follow the advice in this book.

---

2. If you earn between $50,000 and $150,000, you are getting by. Your bills are paid and you can afford some small luxuries, but you have to be careful.
3. When your family income exceeds $150,000, you are affluent. That means you can live as well as the richest man on earth. The only difference will be the price of your toys.

If you can get your income above $150,000 a year and curb your enthusiasm for expensive toys, the chances that you'll be wealthy one day are about 99.9 percent.

HOW MUCH WEALTH DO YOU NEED?

Having a personal net worth of 10 times the amount you need to live on is, in my opinion, an adequate amount of wealth.

What it means is that if you earn an average of 10 percent on your savings, you'll be able to spend what you need for your lifestyle (barring financial emergencies) and never have to dip into your financial nest egg (your savings).

That's a good goal: to squirrel away an amount of money big enough to let you live off the interest. But how much money? At what rate of interest?

Historically, the stock market has returned an average of about 10 percent per year. If you are a middle-of-the-road investor (and by that I'm referring to your temperament, level of optimism, and tolerance of risk), you may feel good about putting all your money into a middle-of-the-road index fund—which is a way to get average stock market returns over a longer period of time.

If, however, you are more adventurous, you may find yourself investing in individual stocks, shooting for a higher return— possibly in the 15 percent to 18 percent range.

If you are very conservative, as I am, you may put most of your money in some sort of safe bond portfolio that will give you only a 4 percent to 6 percent return on your investment (ROI) over time.

Later in this book, I'm going to try to convince you to boost your ROIs by doing two things:

1. Investing in real estate (even now you can do it safely), which could easily give you a safe 25 percent ROI.

2. Investing in your own businesses, which can provide you with a 35 percent to 50 percent ROI in each case.

By combining real estate and small businesses into your investment mix, you could, I believe, easily achieve an overall ROI of between 12 percent and 25 percent.

We'll explore this more in Chapter 2. Right now, let's figure out how much income you will need to maintain your ideal lifestyle. And then let's determine what kind of ROI you feel comfortable expecting from your savings.

LIFESTYLE LEVELS FOR INCOMES ABOVE $150,000

Since you don't have a lot of life experience yet, here's a shortcut to help you figure out what would be the ideal income level for you:

- *$150,000 to $350,000:* You have all you need and all you want. Your toys are modest. Your vacations are great.
- *$350,000 to $1 million:* You have everything you need and want. Your toys are elaborate, and your vacations are insane.
- *$1 million or more:* You have too much income.

In picking your income goal, keep in mind that you may have to work harder—and you will almost certainly encounter more stress—as you move up the income ladder. So aim for a number that is on the modest side of what you are willing to accept. Personally, I don't think anyone needs a lifestyle that's richer than what he or she could enjoy on an income of between $150,000 and $350,000.

ECOLOGY MEETS PROFIT

When 21-year-old Thomas Szaky and fellow classmate Jon Beyer—also 21—developed a business plan for the 2002 Princeton Business Plan competition, they had no idea it would turn into a million-dollar venture. Wanting to do something good for the environment, they developed an organic plant fertilizer—TerraCycle—that is made entirely out of worm waste and is even packaged in recycled soda bottles. (Szaky and Beyer collected the bottles from students and bottling plants all over North America.)

Although they placed fourth in 2002, the TerraCycle team went on to win the 2003 competition, a cash award of $5,000. They then entered and won the Carrot Capital Business Plan Challenge, and a chance to collect $1 million in venture capital.

Szaky and Beyer did plenty of hard—and dirty—work to make their product succeed. Part of their project included gathering tons of rotting trash from a university cafeteria. They then turned the trash into compost through a process known as vericomposting—where it is finely chopped, placed in a heated container to kill pathogens, and digested and excreted by worms.

The eco-friendly plant fertilizer can already be found in some U.S. stores, including Whole Foods, Shop Rite, and Wegmans. In addition, TerraCycle has landed an account with Wal-Mart Canada Corporation, with projected sales of $3 million.

> While working with plant fertilizer was a "total fluke," Szaky says he is happy where it has landed him. And he encourages other hopeful entrepreneurs to diverge from the traditional path. "It's worth doing something unexpected," Szaky said. "Surprise yourself."
>
> *Source:* Marina Strauss, "Young Entrepreneur Wiggled His Way into Wal-Mart," *GlobeandMail.com*, February 4, 2005.

But you decide. Write that number down on a piece of paper. Now take that number and multiply it by your projected ROI:

1. If you are conservative and pessimistic, project 8 percent.
2. If you are aggressive and optimistic, project 13 percent.
3. If you're somewhere in between, project a figure between 9 percent and 17 percent.

When you multiply the first number (the amount of income you figure you'll need to enjoy your ideal life) by the second number (the ROI that feels right to you), you'll come up with the amount of money you will need to have in savings in order to achieve financial independence.

This is a somewhat oversimplified formula, but it will do for now. At this point, your main goal should be to establish your major financial goals and get to work on achieving them. There will be plenty of time later to tweak our formula to account for inflation, taxes, and so on.

But by completing this initial calculation, you have already accomplished more—in terms of wealth building—than most people ever accomplish. Congratulations!

Now, let's move on to the really fun stuff—discovering the secrets of making wealth automatic!

CHAPTER 2

STARTING YOUNG: HOW TO TAKE ADVANTAGE OF THE "MIRACLE" OF COMPOUND INTEREST

"THE MOST POWERFUL FORCE IN THE UNIVERSE"

Legend has it that Albert Einstein was once asked what he considered the most powerful force in the universe. He answered, "Compound interest!"

It's commonly thought that Einstein was joking when he made that famous pronouncement. I'd like to think he was serious. Compound interest is indeed one of the most powerful forces in the universe of making money. But it's also—as we'll see later in this book—one of the most profoundly powerful forces in every area of human enterprise.

Whether your goal is to create a new vaccine, build a faster computer, design a better building, or eliminate poverty, the time and effort you *invest* in your goals will compound over time, providing you with increasingly greater rewards as time passes.

That's a good thing to keep in mind when we talk about choosing a career, getting your first job, and enjoying a successful career. Right now, let's take a look at how compound interest works for your wealth-building goals.

HOW TO TURN A PENNY INTO $21.4 MILLION

If you took a penny and doubled it every day for a month, how much would you come up with? A hundred dollars? A thousand dollars? How about a million dollars?

Not even close. If you start with just a single penny and double it every day for 31 days, you'll end up with . . . $21,474,836.48. Over twenty-one million dollars in a single month! This is an example of the power of compound interest.

Your original penny will have turned into two. But then those two will have turned into four, those four turned into eight, and so on. The growth of your money will have *accelerated,* or sped up, not only because your original penny was collecting interest but also because all the pennies you received as interest also began to earn interest. And so the growth built up—or *compounded.*

That's how we get the term *compound interest.* That's how you get rich. And that's why, when it comes to wealth building, your age gives you a major advantage.

There are three components to compound interest:

1. How much you invest
2. What return you get on your investment
3. How many years you stay invested

KEEP YOUR COOL ON YOUR WAY UP

Shakespeare said that there are seven stages of life:

Infancy

Youth

Stepping into Adulthood

Beginning the Climb to the Top

The Achievement of the Success

The Golden Years

The Final Years

As a recent graduate, you are in the fourth stage—at which you leave your romantic illusions behind and set out on a serious course of making a living, raising a family, and achieving your goals.

This is an exciting time of life, when many good things can happen. But because you are in this stage now, you may find yourself occasionally making the same mistakes Shakespeare warned against in *As You Like It:* "Jealous in honour, sudden and quick in quarrel, / Seeking the bubble reputation . . ." In other words, you may find that it's sometimes hard to stay humble and too easy to get into arguments.

It's not easy to maintain a cordial demeanor and avoid making enemies as you climb your way to the top, but it can be done. By adding gratefulness to the other interpersonal skills you're developing during this period, you'll be doubly blessed.

I'll come back to these three components over and over again throughout this book, because they are the fundamentals of wealth building. If you understand that, then you can take a look at the way this book is organized and see how wealth can be developed automatically by your doing the following things:

1. Starting to invest this year and investing more every year till you're rich
2. Discovering ways to earn above-average returns on your savings
3. Saving first and living comfortably off the balance so that your wealth can accumulate undisturbed till you are wealthy enough to stop working

As you will soon see (if you don't know it already), the more years you invest, the faster your wealth will build. It's a geometric equation, with each year's wealth building more rapidly than did the wealth you had the year before. At some point in time, it is racing forward like a runaway train. That is why rich people so often get richer. It's not that they are smarter than everyone else; it's just that they've taken advantage of compound interest.

So the key is time. And at your age, time is on your side.

It's true. Because you are so young, you can take full advantage of compound interest via the process of saving (or investing) money over a long period of time. The idea in a nutshell: If you invest a modest amount of money over a long period of time, you can become very wealthy.

I'm going to show you how miraculous compound interest is. When you see what I have to show you, you'll be astonished. By putting this miracle to work for you now, you can become very, very wealthy by the time you are ready to retire. It's virtually guaranteed.

At your age, it may sometimes feel like time is dragging. As you get older—as your parents have surely told you countless times—it seems to speed up. By the time you are married with children, time will be racing along . . . and you'll hardly even notice it. One day—and when this happens, it will seem like today was yesterday—you'll be attending graduation ceremonies for your own children.

When that day comes, you may be poor, financially comfortable, or very wealthy. It's entirely up to you.

Yes, it's up to you. Despite what some of your college profs may have told you, it doesn't take privilege, rich parents, or great connections to acquire and enjoy wealth. All it takes is three things:

1. The discipline to save money before you spend it
2. The ability to invest that saved money at a decent rate of return
3. The good fortune to live a full life

Those are the only things involved. As we'll see in a minute, if you start saving a reasonable percentage of your income now and continue to do so until you are retired (that would be in about 40 or 45 years), you'll certainly be rich. It will be easy— virtually automatic!

The purpose of this chapter is to convince you to begin saving money immediately by showing you how miraculously those savings build up as time passes.

Are you ready to be convinced? Okay, let's take a look at how miraculous compound interest can be.

We will begin with an assumption that probably isn't true—that you have $30,000 in your bank account right now. (Don't worry, the Automatic Wealth program for graduates doesn't expect you to have any cash now. But right now, for the purpose of illustrating the power of compound interest, just imagine that you do have 30 grand to spend as you wish.)

One thing you could do with that $30,000 would be to buy a new car—say, a BMW 3 Series sedan. Having a car like

TABLE 2.1

Estimated Depreciation of a Brand-New $30,000 Vehicle	
Year	Value after 15% annual depreciation (25% for the first 3 years)
0	$30,000.00 (purchase price)
1	$22,500.00
5	$9,144.14
10	$4,057.30
15	$1,800.25
20	$798.78

that would definitely provide you with a good deal of fun and a sexy way to get to and from your first job. But what would it do to your wealth-building prospects?

Let's take a look. Table 2.1 shows what would happen to that $30,000, in terms of the resale value of the BMW, over a 20-year period.

You can see from the table that when you walk out of the showroom, the value of your new car is instantly diminished by almost $8,000. That means, in effect, that you'd be $8,000 poorer. Five years later, you'd have lost another $13,000. And by the time you were in your early 40s, your car would be worth no more than its weight in scrap metal.

This decline in value over time is something financial people call *depreciation*.

In terms of your future wealth, investing that $30,000 in a new BMW was not a great choice. Yes, you had the fun of driving a brand-new Beamer. But you could probably have had just as much fun and gotten richer, instead of poorer, by making a different choice.

A QUESTION TO ASK YOURSELF WHENEVER YOU'RE ABOUT TO BUY OR SELL ANYTHING

Here's an important thing to know (and if you can remember this for the rest of your life, it will always help you make good financial decisions). When you buy something, you are almost always immediately poorer. When you buy a new BMW, for example, it *depreciates* (loses value) the moment you drive it out of the showroom. Investing in something—such as a stock portfolio—is a purchase, too. The difference is that cars are usually depreciating assets (they lose value over time) whereas stocks—good stocks, at least—are appreciating assets (meaning that they increase in value over time). Every time you get yourself into a buy/sell transaction, ask yourself these questions: "What am I doing right now in terms of my wealth?" and "Am I getting richer or poorer?" Forget for a moment how the transaction makes you feel emotionally—because that can change. Focus on the impact it has on your wealth (net worth). If you can teach yourself to ask these questions habitually, you will make much wiser decisions.

Let's imagine that instead of buying that new BMW you purchased an older model—essentially the same car, but just five years older. And let's say you invested in the stock market the $10,000 you saved by not buying the new BMW. Your five-year-old BMW would continue to depreciate, just as the new one would—but the rate would be less dramatic, because the big haircut (jargon for *depreciation* or *discount*) would already be a *fait accompli*. While your car depreciates, however, your stock investment appreciates. For the purpose of this discussion, we are going to assume that you put your money into a no-load mutual fund that tracks a major stock index. Such an investment could reasonably be expected to return at least 10 percent a year over 20 years.

Table 2.2 shows what your wealth situation would look like if you did that.

Deciding to enjoy a slightly older BMW and invest the difference would have made you a lot richer down the line— almost $70,000 richer, according to Table 2.2. That's a lot. But let's take this a step further and imagine that you let that original $10,000 investment work for you long after the BMW was gone. Let's say you kept it in some sort of a no-load mutual fund yielding 10 percent. What would you have then?

You can find the answer yourself by going on the Internet and using a compound-interest calculator. (I like www.1728.com/compint.htm.)

If we assume you are 22 years old now and kept the $10,000 in an account giving you a 10 percent ROI over 43 years, you'd have gotten $602,400.69 richer. That's more than a half million dollars in wealth that you didn't have to work for!

TABLE 2.2

Estimated Depreciation of a 5-Year-Old $20,000 Vehicle		Compound Interest at 10% Annual Returns	
Year	Value after 15% depreciation	Year	Value after 10% return
0	$20,000.00 (purchase price)	0	$10,000.00 (initial investment)
1	$17,000.00	1	$11,000.00
5	$8,874.11	5	$16,105.10
10	$3,937.49	10	$25,937.42
15	$1,747.08	15	$41,772.48
20	$775.19	20	$67,275.00

You can see the point I'm making, can't you? If you spend $30,000 on a BMW now, you may feel good momentarily—but in 20 years, you'll be $77,000 poorer than you would be if you were smarter now. And that difference is the result of a one-time investment. Just think how much wealthier you'd be if you continually added to that investment.

Think about this. In 40 years, you will be about 60 years old. I know that seems ancient to you now, but when you are 60 you will probably still be very vital, very healthy, and very much interested in enjoying your life. Imagine how much better your life would be then if you had—in addition to a family and career that you love—all the money you could ever possibly need . . . and then some!

If you start saving and investing your money now, that day will come. It's virtually guaranteed.

For the miracle of compound interest to work its wonders, you need 30 or 40 years of savings. And as a young person, you have the advantage of that much time.

You will be 60 years old one day. When that day comes, most of the people you went to school with will still be struggling to pay their bills. If you don't do anything about wealth

---

WHAT IF YOU HAVE MORE IMPORTANT GOALS THAN GETTING RICH?

As I pointed out in Chapter 1, there is nothing in the Automatic Wealth program that will stop you from doing what you want in life—from, say, pursuing your dreams and having fun. My wealth-building system allows you to do all of that while you are simultaneously building up a fortune.

building now, you may find yourself struggling with them. But if you start now, by taking advantage of compound interest, you will never have to struggle—not now and not ever.

Could you get rich without the miracle of compound interest? Yes, you could. You *could* win the lottery one day. You *could* get discovered and become a rock star. You *could* build your house on top of a hidden gold mine. And you *could* give a hitchhiker a ride and inherit his fortune.

That *could* happen. But it probably won't.

If you commit yourself to the Automatic Wealth plan now, you won't have to worry. You'll have your cake (a multimillion-dollar bank account) and eat it too (enjoy your life and career). It's entirely up to you.

START SAVING THE MINUTE YOU GRADUATE

To take full advantage of the miracle of compound interest, you must begin to save and invest immediately—as soon as you start earning an income. Saving money when you are starting out may seem difficult at first. After all, you have got plenty of bills to pay (including, perhaps, college loans) and your income, as a new worker, isn't likely to be very high.

Still, I recommend that you set an aggressive goal for yourself: to save 15 percent of your pretax income. Saving 15 percent of your income when you are just starting out might sound like a challenge. It is. But if you are willing to make some reasonable sacrifices (such as sharing an apartment and driving a used car), you'll be able to do it. Later in this book, I'll show you how to "live rich" on a budget. Right now, let's see what happens when you save 15 percent of your income during your entire working career.

AN AVERAGE INCOME PLUS AVERAGE RETURNS CAN EQUAL ABOVE-AVERAGE WEALTH

Let's review what we said earlier in this chapter. There are three keys to building wealth through compound interest:

1. How much you invest
2. How long you invest
3. What kind of return you get on your investments

How much you can invest depends on two things: how much you earn and how much you spend. Earnings for college graduates vary, but the average starting salary for grads in 2005, according to the National Association of Colleges and Employers, is $30,337. (You can check out the data yourself by visiting www.naceweb.org.)

Later in this book, I'll show you how to dramatically increase your earnings. For the purposes of this exercise, we are going to assume that you are beginning with an average salary and that it increases at an average rate.

How long you invest is up to you. But to show you the miracle of compound interest, we are going to assume that you start saving now and continue until you're 65. (If you follow all of the principles in this book, you'll probably get wealthy way before you are 65. But that doesn't mean you won't keep saving. You probably will. Once you have the saving habit, it's hard to break.)

What you earn on your savings depends on what type of investing you do. If you invest in the stock market—which is the way most people invest—you can expect to make between 10 percent and 13 percent on your money. Let me explain those numbers.

Stock market historians will tell you that the average ROI of the Standard & Poor's (S&P) 500 (an index of 500 of the largest companies in the United States) from 1950 to 2000 was 13.2 percent. That encompasses nine *bear* (losing) markets, including the big bear market of the 1970s and the crash of 1987. But it also includes today's stock market, which, in the view of some analysts, is overvalued (too pricey). Because of that, conservative stock analysts prefer to use a longer average—the measure of how stocks have performed since the beginning of the century. If you go back that far, the average ROI for the stock market is about 10 percent.

Now let's say that you start making an average income the minute you get out of school. According to the National Association of Colleges and Employers, as mentioned earlier, that would be $30,337 a year. And let's say that you are good at your job, so you get consistent annual raises of 4 percent. So you'd be making $43,179 a year 10 years from now, and $140,046 in 40 years. You'll not only be making more money but also will be able to save more money. If you consistently— that means every year—deposit 15 percent of your income into investments, compound interest will begin to accumulate in a way you wouldn't believe.

I'm about to show you three tables that may blow you away. They all assume that you start out with an average income for a college graduate and that your income increases at an average rate. They all assume, too, that you save and invest 15 percent of your income.

Table 2.3—the most conservative of the three—shows how much money you would acquire if your investments returned only 10 percent a year.

Pretty interesting, huh? Just by investing 15 percent of your income and having a very ordinary income-earning life, you'd be worth about $5.5 million when you are ready to retire. If

TABLE 2.3

**Example of Wealth Built Up by an Investor at a 10% Rate
of Return with a 4% Annual Increase in Income**

Year	Age	Income	Deposit (15% of income)	Interest	Total Value of Investment
1	22	$30,337.00	$4,550.55	$455.06	$5,005.61
5	26	$35,490.00	$5,323.50	$2,987.11	$32,858.22
10	31	$43,179.01	$6,476.85	$8,445.05	$92,895.53
15	36	$52,533.87	$7,880.08	$18,022.49	$198,247.38
20	41	$63,915.48	$9,587.32	$34,405.02	$378,455.17
25	46	$77,762.96	$11,664.44	$61,954.75	$681,502.24
30	51	$94,610.53	$14,191.58	$107,741.89	$1,185,160.81
35	56	$115,108.77	$17,266.23	$183,207.78	$2,015,285.59
40	61	$140,045.69	$21,007.00	$306,845.37	$3,375,299.05
45	66	$170,388.22	$25,558.23	$508,518.71	$5,593,705.86
50	71	$207,303.32	$31,095.50	$836,422.71	$9,200,649.84
55	76	$252,216.19	$37,832.43	$1,368,295.59	$15,051,251.52

you decided to work an extra 10 years, till you were 75, you'd be worth $15 million!

Take a moment to note how your net worth, which is represented by the column labeled "Total Value of Investment," accelerates after year 30. Until then, your wealth is building steadily but is nothing to brag about. At the 30-year mark, when you are about 51, you become a millionaire. Every year thereafter, it starts to really move.

Now let's take a look at Table 2.4, which shows the same situation with only one difference: It assumes you are able to get an ROI of 13 percent. As I explained, that was the average stock market return from 1950 to 2000.

As you can see, a 13 percent ROI will bring your net worth

TABLE 2.4

**Example of Wealth Built Up by an Investor at a 13.2%
Rate of Return with a 4% Annual Increase in Income**

Year	Age	Income	Deposit (15% of Income)	Interest	Total Value of Investment
1	22	$30,337.00	$4,550.55	$600.67	$5,151.22
5	26	$35,490.00	$5,323.50	$4,192.60	$35,954.68
10	31	$43,179.01	$6,476.85	$12,894.12	$110,576.86
15	36	$52,533.87	$7,880.08	$30,173.63	$258,761.73
20	41	$63,915.48	$9,587.32	$63,637.30	$545,738.07
25	46	$77,762.96	$11,664.44	$127,475.36	$1,093,197.82
30	51	$94,610.53	$14,191.58	$248,127.69	$2,127,882.94
35	56	$115,108.17	$17,266.23	$474,817.45	$4,071,919.33
40	61	$140,046.69	$21,007.00	$899,133.95	$7,710,754.80
45	66	$170,388.22	$25,558.23	$1,691,436.89	$14,505,352.72
50	71	$207,303.32	$31,095.50	$3,168,528.75	$27,172,534.39
55	76	$252,216.19	$37,832.43	$5,919,449.50	$50,763,763.90

up to $15 million by the time you are 65—and if you keep saving till you are 75, you'll be worth 50 million bucks!

I know these numbers seem incredible, but we are just warming up. Now let's assume that you become a savvy investor and earn 18 percent on your savings. Is that possible? Indeed it is.

A colleague of mine, James O'Shaughnessy, studied the results of various investment strategies from 1952 to 1994. In his great book *What Works on Wall Street* (McGraw-Hill, 1996), he reported that investing in stocks with the lowest price-to-sales and high earnings growth rates posted compounded annual average returns of 18.4 percent during that period. When he updated the figures two years later, he found that the performance of this strategy had actually improved, producing 18.81 percent annual returns between 1952 and 1996.

His study was completed before the Internet bubble popped. If he brought it up to date today, the ROI might be lower. But there are other studies that demonstrate that it's possible to achieve that kind of return.

One was done by Christopher Graja and Dr. Elizabeth Ungar. For their book *Investing in Small-Cap Stocks* (revised edition, Bloomberg Press, 1999), they looked at the performance of different types of small caps (stocks with total market values in the bottom quintile, or lowest 20 percent, of the market) from 1975 to 1997. They found that small-cap value stocks returned about 18 percent during that time.

More recently, I've seen programs by stock experts Porter Stansberry and Steve Sjuggerud that have shown consistent, longer-term ROI projections at this level using other stock selection methods.

The secret to getting above-average returns with stocks, the market analysts say, is to apply a good system consistently. Too many investors jump from one stock program to another in a vain effort to maximize their profits. History tells us it is much better to find one system that works and stick with it.

We'll talk more later on about getting good returns on stocks. The purpose of this chapter isn't to sell you on stock investing but to show you what can happen if you start investing 15 percent of your income now and keep doing so till you are rich enough to retire.

I've selected three sample ROIs—10 percent, 13 percent, and 18.8 percent—with some justification. This is not to argue for stocks but to demonstrate what a giant difference a 3 percent to 9 percent spread on your ROI can make.

Is 18 percent too much to hope for? I don't think so. And after we take a look at the next table, I'll tell you why. But right now, let's get back to looking at what would happen if you invested 15 percent of your income over time at an 18.8 percent ROI. See Table 2.5.

So what do you think of that? You'll be worth a million at age 41, $6 million at 51, $15 million at 56, $35 million at 61, and $200 million by the time you are 71!

These may seem like fantasy numbers, but they are not. This is the literal truth of what would happen if you started investing right now.

If, by the way, you've ever wondered how the super-rich get so rich, take a look at how the net worth numbers (the last column of the chart) accelerate after year 30: Six becomes 15

TABLE 2.5

**Example of Wealth Built Up by an Investor at an 18.8%
Rate of Return with a 4% Annual Increase in Income**

Year	Age	Income	Deposit (15% of Income)	Interest	Total Value of Investment
1	22	$30,337.00	$4,550.55	$855.50	$5,406.05
5	26	$35,490.00	$5,323.50	$6,645.84	$41,996.07
10	31	$43,179.01	$6,476.85	$23,812.19	$150,472.79
15	36	$52,533.87	$7,880.08	$66,185.87	$418,238.38
20	41	$63,915.48	$9,587.32	$168,588.89	$1,065,338.28
25	46	$77,762.96	$11,664.44	$413,505.13	$2,613,000.52
30	51	$94,610.53	$14,191.58	$996,221.86	$6,295,274.32
35	56	$115,108.17	$17,266.23	$2,378,982.21	$15,033,142.90
40	61	$140,046.69	$21,007.00	$5,655,771.42	$35,739,661.93
45	66	$170,388.22	$25,558.23	$13,415,540.84	$84,774,800.65
50	71	$207,303.32	$31,095.50	$31,784,920.20	$200,853,644.68
55	76	$252,216.19	$37,832.43	$75,262,034.00	$475,592,002.06

in five years, and then 15 becomes 35, and then 35 becomes 84, and then 84 becomes 200, and then 200 becomes 475!

GET EVEN HIGHER ROIs THE AUTOMATIC WEALTH WAY

I'm presuming you are blown away, as I am every time I look at numbers like these. The skeptic in me jumps out and challenges the assumptions:

1. *How much you invest.* Are the invested amounts realistic? In my opinion, they are conservative. Any college graduate with discipline can learn to save 15 percent of his or her income. And if you follow the advice I'll give you later on, your income will appreciate much faster than the 4 percent per year figure I used for these charts.

2. *How long you invest.* That is not a debatable point. It's simply a matter of mathematics. If you are indeed 22 years old now and you do indeed invest until you are 65, the 43-year duration used here will be accurate. As I've tried to make abundantly clear, compound interest becomes astounding after about 30 years of investing. That's why you have such a great advantage when you start young. (That means right now!)

3. *What ROI you get.* You may not be able to earn 18.8 percent on your stocks throughout your entire life. But if you learn how to invest in local real estate—which is something you can do even now in a highly overvalued real estate market—you can expect to earn about 30 percent on that. And if you start your own successful

business one day (and there's no better time than the present), you may well see investment returns of 50 percent or more over time.

As I will explain later, the average appreciation for real estate is about 5 percent or 6 percent depending on which sources you go to. If you leverage (ratchet up) those percentages by financing your real estate purchases (with mortgages), you can expect those returns to be four or five times higher. Moreover, if you are careful about buying under the market by 4 percent or 5 percent, an average ROI of 30 percent a year is not unrealistic.

Putting aside, for the moment, the 50-plus percent returns you could hope to get by starting your own business, let's see what would happen if you invested a portion of your savings in stocks, where you got only a 10 percent return, and another portion in real estate, where you averaged, with leverage, the expected 30 percent ROI. (Again, we will assume that you start with an ordinary income that increases at an ordinary rate and that you save 15 percent of it.) See Table 2.6.

In Table 2.6, we have added one column of 10 percent returns (on half of the 15 percent of your income that you set aside for investments) and one column of 30 percent returns (on the other half of that 15 percent of your income). If we add the interest together, we find that you will reach $2 million before your forty-first birthday. If you still choose to retire at 65, your investments will have bloomed to approximately $1.1 billion. And at age 76, you will have over $21 billion in accumulated interest.

Look, I know these numbers are mind-boggling. You might be experiencing a little skepticism right now. Perhaps you're wondering, "If it's so easy to amass such a fortune, why isn't everyone rich?"

TABLE 2.6

Example of Wealth Built Up by an Investor with Half of His or Her Deposit at 10% ROI and Half of His or Her Deposit at 30% ROI

Year	Age	Income (with a 4% Annual Increase)	Deposit (15% of Income)	Interest 10%	Total 10%	Interest 30%	Total 30%	Total Value of Investment
1	22	$30,337.00	$4,550.55	$227.53	$2,502.80	$682.58	$2,957.86	$5,460.66
5	26	$35,490.00	$5,323.50	$1,493.56	$16,429.11	$6,553.52	$28,398.58	$44,827.69
10	31	$43,179.01	$6,476.85	$4,222.52	$46,447.77	$32,306.12	$139,993.18	$186,440.94
15	36	$52,533.87	$7,880.08	$9,011.24	$99,123.69	$129,651.16	$561,821.70	$660,945.39
20	41	$63,915.48	$9,587.32	$17,202.51	$189,227.59	$493,188.21	$2,137,148.91	$2,326,376.50
25	46	$77,762.96	$11,664.44	$30,977.37	$340,751.12	$1,845,532.87	$7,997,309.09	$8,338,060.22
30	51	$94,610.53	$14,191.58	$53,870.95	$592,580.40	$6,869,804.96	$29,769,154.83	$30,361,735.24
35	56	$115,108.17	$17,266.23	$91,603.89	$1,007,642.80	$25,528,360.61	$110,622,895.96	$111,630,538.75
40	61	$140,046.69	$21,007.00	$153,422.68	$1,687,649.53	$94,810,876.71	$410,847,132.42	$412,534,781.95
45	66	$170,388.22	$25,558.23	$254,259.36	$2,796,852.93	$352,057,612.06	$1,525,582,985.58	$1,528,379,838.51
50	71	$207,303.32	$31,095.50	$418,211.36	$4,600,324.92	$1,307,203,549.79	$5,664,548,715.77	$5,669,149,040.69
55	76	$252,216.19	$37,832.43	$684,147.80	$7,525,625.76	$4,853,601,849.92	$21,032,274,683.01	$21,039,800,308.77

The answer is that few people do what I suggest. Few put away a consistent amount of income. Few do start young. Few stay invested in a consistently conservative stock portfolio. But the people who do it *do* become this wealthy.

You will also have to remember that this huge amount won't be quite as much in 43 years as it is today. In today's dollars, $8 billion would probably be just over $1 billion (estimating a 4 percent annual rate of inflation). That's still an unthinkable amount of money.

But now I want you to go even further.

SUPERCHARGE YOUR SAVINGS BY RADICALLY INCREASING YOUR INCOME

In all of the tables we've looked at so far, the assumption has been that your income will increase only 4 percent a year. That's what happens to ordinary income earners. That's not necessarily what will happen to you. By following the Automatic Wealth for Graduates program, you can expect income increases that are much greater than that. For starters, I'll give you ways to get your income up to $150,000 a year within three or four years. Perhaps more important, I will show you how to become an invaluable employee so that you can expect to see salary increases of at least 5 percent a year.

High-income earners make most of their money by practicing a single skill within the context of a single industry. Don't be fooled by financial gurus who tell you otherwise. But high earners eventually develop *many* streams of income. And I'm going to argue that you should do the same thing.

To get your financial fortune started, you have to radically boost your income. And doing that, as I'll explain in Chapter 5, requires doing one thing extraordinarily well.

In the second part of Chapter 6, we will talk about many ways that you can supplement your primary income. I'll show you how to start small and develop extra little streams of cash that happily float into your bank account every month and build up your wealth reserve.

Many master wealth builders that I know enjoy a dozen sources of income. Some are modest; some are amazing. That's the great thing about creating cash flow. Although you never know what will happen with any individual source of income, one will turn into a river if you get enough of them started.

HOW INCREASING YOUR INCOME CAN ADD TO YOUR NET SAVINGS

As I have said, studies show that good employees can expect to earn salary increases of about 4 percent a year. Extraordinary employees can do better than that. If you follow the advice given in later chapters, you can easily get a 5 percent increase in salary per year. Let's see what that would mean in terms of how big a salary you can expect, over time. See Table 2.7. Note that I've calculated this only until age 51. That's because salaries tend to top out at that age and that level. Still, you can see how much of a difference it can make to get 5 percent instead of 4 percent.

If you start off with a normal salary now and do nothing more than get a mere 5 percent per annum increase, you'll be making six figures in less than 25 years and nearly half a million dollars if you continue to work into your 70s.

There's one more wrinkle. As your income increases—if you maintain your lifestyle but don't increase your spending by too much—you'll get wealthier faster. You can also save

TABLE 2.7

Income of an Extraordinary Employee

Year	Age	Income (with 5% Annual Increase)
1	22	$30,337.00
5	26	$36,874.81
10	31	$47,062.64
15	36	$60,065.18
20	41	$76,660.09
25	46	$97,839.86
30	51	$124,871.21

more. If you increase your savings rate by 1 percent every five years—even if you revert to the most conservative investment strategy I used earlier in this chapter—you can see how your wealth thrives. Look at Table 2.8.

Table 2.8 shows that 40 years from now, when you're just 4 years from retirement, you'll have over $4 million. At 71, you'll have about $12.5 million. If you work even harder to increase your income and reach that $150,000 mark by age 25, you'll have your first million dollars by the time you're 38.

But this is just the beginning. Using the methods in this book, you could quite possibly be making a cool million in as few as seven years after you hit that $150,000 mark.

In Table 2.9, look at how increasing your income to $1 million in seven years can skyrocket your bank account.

While earning an average income with a 5 percent annual increase, you were able to reach $1 million only after about 28 years of saving. But when you radically increase your income— as Table 2.9 indicates—you can save over $1 million by the time you're 34 . . . only 12 years from now. And look how

TABLE 2.8

Example of Wealth Built Up by an Investor at a 10% Rate of Return When Increasing His or Her Deposit by 1% of His or Her Income Every 5 Years

Year	Age	Income (with 5% Annual Increase)	Deposit	Interest	Total Value of Investment
1	22	$30,337.00	$4,550.55	$455.06	$5,005.61
5	26	$36,874.81	$5,531.22	$3,041.85	$33,460.31
10	31	$47,062.64	$7,530.02	$9,039.99	$99,439.93
15	36	$60,065.18	$10,211.08	$20,174.49	$221,919.43
20	41	$76,660.09	$13,798.82	$40,079.76	$440,877.36
25	46	$97,839.86	$18,589.57	$74,772.02	$822,492.27
30	51	$124,871.21	$24,974.24	$134,155.46	$1,475,710.01
35	56	$159,370.82	$33,467.87	$234,464.06	$2,579,104.68
40	61	$203,402.04	$44,748.45	$402,215.73	$4,424,373.01
45	66	$259,598.27	$59,707.60	$680,608.12	$7,486,689.29
50	71	$331,320.48	$79,516.92	$1,139,855.80	$12,538,413.81

quickly your wealth continues to build. You'll have nearly $177 million by the time you're 71!

Even if you take a little longer to increase your income, you can still end up with tremendous wealth. For example, look at the following possibilities:

- If you're making $150,000 by age 31 and $1 million by 38, you'll have net savings of $110 million by age 71.
- If you're making $150,000 by age 29 and $1 million by 36, you'll have net savings of $122 million by age 71.

By taking steps to drastically improve your income and consistently investing 15 percent or more, you will retire a multimillionaire.

TABLE 2.9

Example of Wealth Built Up by an Investor at a 10% Rate
of Return When Increasing His or Her Deposit by 1%
of His or Her Income Every 5 Years

Year	Age	Income (with 5% Annual Increase)	Deposit	Interest	Total Value of Investment
1	22	$30,337.00	$4,550.55	$455.06	$5,005.61
5	26	$157,500.00	$23,625.00	$6,746.76	$74,214.39
10	31	$201,014.35	$32,162.30	$28,553.10	$314,084.08
15	36	$1,215,506.25	$206,636.06	$159,622.72	$1,755,849.90
20	41	$1,551,328.22	$279,239.08	$410,639.04	$4,517,029.42
25	46	$1,979,931.60	$376,187.00	$868,218.98	$9,550,408.79
30	51	$2,526,950.20	$505,390.04	$1,676,210.12	$18,438,311.30
35	56	$3,225,099.94	$677,270.99	$3,072,012.33	$33,792,135.59
40	61	$4,116,135.60	$905,549.83	$5,445,505.67	$59,900,562.32
45	66	$5,253,347.97	$1,208,270.03	$9,434,518.71	$103,779,705.82
50	71	$6,704,751.15	$1,609,140.28	$16,079,319.14	$176,872,510.58

THE SNOWBALL (OR "DOUGHBALL") EFFECT

As you can see from the preceding tables, compound interest begins to work for you right away. The second year, you're already making more interest than you did the first year; the third year, you're making more than you did the second year; and so on . . . even though you're always receiving the same interest rate. As a result of the compounding, your investment grows geometrically over time—like a snowball rolling down a hill, becoming bigger and bigger.

The longer you stay the course, in other words, the more your wealth increases. That's why time is your greatest strength as a young investor. You have your whole life ahead of you. And that means you can take maximum advantage of the power of compound interest.

By investing 15 percent of your income starting with your first paycheck, and getting slightly higher than average raises, you can get wealthy quickly—and very, very wealthy by the time your friends and colleagues start to think about planning for retirement.

START SAVING TODAY

Starting today—literally, today—begin the practice of saving.

Even if you just started working and feel overwhelmed by the college loans you have to pay back, you must start your saving program today. You must get your hands on some amount of money and invest it immediately. Start with 15 percent of your gross income. If you don't have that much cash, put away as much as you possibly can.

The reason you want to start saving now, even if your income is small, is that you want to create the *habit* of saving.

When saving becomes habitual, it becomes easier. And anything that you can do easily, you'll do better, more often, and over a longer term. The result, over time, will be significant compounding wealth.

PAY YOURSELF FIRST—AFTER UNCLE SAM

According to MoneyChimp.com, a person who makes $30,337 is right on the bottom edge of the 25 percent tax bracket. Because the government pays itself first, by taking withholding taxes out of your paycheck, you'll see only your after-tax income, which will be $22,753. You have to make sure to pay yourself next. No matter what, put that $4,550 into a conservative stock portfolio.

You could also put your money into an individual retirement account (IRA) or simplified employee pension (SEP), which will be tax deductible. That will help you grow your wealth faster, because the interest you get on that investment won't be taxed until you spend it—many years from now.

Tax-deferred investments are a plus when it comes to wealth building. But we are not going to talk any more about taxes here. As you've already seen from the preceding tables, you can get plenty rich with or without tax savings. The main thing is to pay out your money in the following order:

1. Pay the government (the IRS and state tax agencies) . . . because they can get very nasty if you don't.
2. Pay yourself—and by that I mean take 15 percent of your income and put it in some sort of an investment.
3. Pay the interest on your debts—credit cards, student loans, car payments, and so on. Keeping that debt low is critical. By paying it third—before your noncritical living expenses—you'll naturally want to keep it to a minimum.
4. Pay for the noncritical parts of your life. Those would include entertainment, travel, and toys.

Once you pay the government and yourself, you will end up with about $18,000 to live on. Sure, $18K isn't a whole lot of money. It leaves you with about $1,500 a month. If, however, you are careful about curbing your spending, you won't have any trouble. You can pay $750 for rent. You may have to split an apartment, but living with other people can be a great experience. You don't *need* to spend $1,000 on rent right now.

A LITTLE SIDE BUSINESS

How old do you have to be to run a company that grosses over $300,000 a year? Scott Smigler proved that you're never too young to be successful. At 22, he was already making six figures with his marketing strategy firm for online businesses, Exclusive Concepts.

Smigler never let his age stand in his way. In fact, he sees his youth as a "huge advantage." Not only was he able to build a lucrative business, he was also able to excel at being a student. He managed to maintain his primary job—attending college—while running Exclusive Concepts from his dorm room. And although he considered leaving school at times in order to devote his full attention to the company, he decided that "it wouldn't be a smart strategy for the long term." He believes that education is critical to business success and growth.

In an interview with the Bentley *Observer,* Smigler notes that entrepreneurial efforts require careful preparation, including a base of "sound principles," a "solid business plan," and "well-thought-out financials." He feels that he is most successful when he focuses on what his company "does best."

Smigler has learned some important lessons since the conception of Exclusive Concepts, especially the value of effective communication. And he cautions entrepreneurs to lead balanced lives—because having fun and having a life separate from your business is necessary and healthy.

Sources: Interview with Maura King Scully, *The Bentley Observer,* www.bentley.edu, Fall 2004; Sarah Pierce, "10 Management Lessons from a Young Entrepreneur," *Entrepreneur,* December 17, 2003.

Setting aside that $250 you save this year won't hurt your lifestyle all that much but it will be worth more to you when you are ready to retire.

In Chapter 9, I'll tell you how to live rich even while you are starting out, struggling to save and invest that 15 percent. Right now, let's review what we've covered in this chapter by way of making a few promises.

If you have come to understand the miracle of compound interest, you'll be very eager to make the following resolutions.

YOUR FIRST AUTOMATIC WEALTH COMMITMENT:
"If I don't have one already, I will get a job that pays me at least $30,000."

YOUR SECOND AUTOMATIC WEALTH COMMITMENT:
"This year and every year for the rest of my working life, I will save at least 15 percent of my gross income."

YOUR THIRD AUTOMATIC WEALTH COMMITMENT:
"I will follow an investment program that gives me a good chance to earn 18 percent to 20 percent a year without taking unnecessary risks."

YOUR FOURTH AUTOMATIC WEALTH COMMITMENT:
"I will reduce the risk involved in earning 18 percent to 20 percent a year by (1) consistently following a proven stock investing program, (2) investing in local real estate, and (3) investing in a private business."

Bonus resolution: There is one more thing you can do to increase the rate at which you will grow rich. This is not required for the Automatic Wealth program, but it helps. You could make a promise to increase your *rate* of saving as your income increases. In other words, instead of sticking with saving 15 percent of your income throughout your career, you could bump your saving rate up as your income goes up. Be careful, though. You can't do this too aggressively. Nor can you do it forever. But if you increase your income every year and hold your expenses down, your savings-to-income ratio can easily get higher. See Table 2.10.

Here are some suggested targets:

More than $30,000 but less than $100,000:   15 percent

More than $100,000 but less than $200,000:   20 percent

More than $200,000 but less than $500,000:   25 percent

More than $1 million but less than $2 million: 35 percent

More than $2 million but less than $5 million: 40 percent

More than $5 million: 45 percent

TABLE 2.10

Income Before and After Taxes and Savings

Income	Tax	Gross Income After Tax	Savings	Income for Living Expenses
$29,700	25%	$22,275	$4,455	$17,820
$71,950	28%	$51,804	$10,793	$41,012
$150,150	33%	$100,601	$30,030	$70,571
$326,450	35%	$212,193	$81,613	$130,580
$1,000,000	35%	$650,000	$350,000	$300,000
$5,000,000	35%	$3,250,000	$2,250,000	$1,000,000
$10,000,000	35%	$6,500,000	$4,500,000	$2,000,000
$50,000,000	35%	$32,500,000	$22,500,000	$10,000,000
$100,000,000	35%	$65,000,000	$45,000,000	$20,000,000
$500,000,000	35%	$325,000,000	$225,000,000	$100,000,000
$1,000,000,000	35%	$650,000,000	$450,000,000	$200,000,000

CHAPTER 3

CHOOSING A REWARDING CAREER: MAKING THE BEST DECISIONS EASILY

They say there are three critical decisions in life:

1. What you choose to do
2. Whom you choose to do it with
3. Where you choose to do it

In this chapter, we are going to talk about the first one: your career.

- How to choose a career
- How to get your first job
- How to rise to the top of your field

I had a tough time choosing a career. I had been working pretty steadily since I was 12 years old and on a full-time basis

WHY HAVING A GOOD AMBITION IS MORE
IMPORTANT THAN HAVING A GOOD JOB

My first son has a great job. At least, it seems like a great job to me. He works in computer engineering. Just two years out of college, he is already earning more than $80,000 a year. That's pretty good money. Not enough to live like a king in Los Angeles—but enough to pay the rent and put 10 percent to 20 percent on the side for savings. Yet despite the creative challenge of developing new ideas and languages, getting great fringe benefits, and making lots of money . . . he's thinking about quitting. Why? Because he doesn't feel like this is what he wants to do. When I ask him what he wants to do, he admits he's not sure. So I've asked him to promise me that he won't quit this job until he's found a better one. And that's the advice I'd give anyone who is in his situation.

My second son has graduated and doesn't have a job. But he knows what he wants to do. He is scraping to get by. (We don't believe in allowing our kids to experience financial dependency. We think it's a very bad and badly addictive habit.) But he's happy. Why is he happy? Because he knows what he wants to do and his heart and mind are filled with ambition.

If you don't know what you want to do, you are going to experience a certain amount of psychological discomfort with any job you have. The problem isn't the job; it's your lack of direction. So my advice to you would be the same as the advice I gave my eldest son: Keep working and saving while you are developing an ambition. How do you develop an ambition if you don't have one? That's a subject big enough for another book—one that I wouldn't do a very good job of writing. But here are just a few ideas to get you started:

- Think back to your childhood. What did you want to do then? Is there still a spark of something left? Could it be ignited?
- Be honest with yourself. Do you have a secret goal that you are not admitting to anyone . . . perhaps not even to yourself? Are you embarrassed to admit that what you really want to do is play professional tennis or dance on Broadway? Let that ambition out of the closet. Even if you lack the resources to accomplish it completely, there are all sorts of adaptations you can probably make that would suit you just fine.
- Make a concentrated effort to figure out what might interest you. Much of this chapter deals with how to do that.
- Spend as little time as possible watching television and playing video games. They steal your time and deaden your imagination. There will be plenty of time to waste on those things once your career is in place. Right now, you owe your life some focused attention.
- If you've plumbed the depths and come up with nothing, don't panic. What I've discovered about career happiness is this: It comes from working hard on something you care about. And there are many things in life you can learn to care about—from pets to police work or poverty, for example. If you simply keep your mind and heart open to the possibilities, something will come.

during my college years, so I'd already experienced a lot of work environments. When I graduated from college, however, I still wasn't sure what I should do.

My secret goal was to become a writer, but the publishing business was in a slump and people weren't hiring. (Even if they had been, I probably wouldn't have gotten a job. I wasn't a good writer at that time.)

Lacking a specific ambition, I pursued a master's degree in English literature at the University of Michigan. I taught freshmen composition in the morning, attended classes in the afternoon, and managed a bar at night.

After completing my master's degree, I was no closer to knowing what I wanted to do—and my dream of being a professional writer seemed just as unattainable as it had two years earlier. So what did I do? I joined the Peace Corps and went off to Africa for two years, where I taught English literature and American philosophy to African students at the University of Chad.

That was a great experience—one I'd recommend to you if this chapter doesn't inspire any other ideas. But I can see now, retrospectively, how clueless I was about picking a career. I was 25 years old, feeling like a full-grown man already, yet I still didn't know how to go about getting the job I really wanted.

So I floundered for a while. Floundered and almost foundered. (Look it up!) Eventually, things worked out. My career halted but then lunged, and eventually I was able to do everything I wanted—and become financially independent along the way. But I do wish someone had sat me down when I was just out of college and given me some direction. That's what I'm hoping to do for you in this chapter.

The ideas and suggestions that follow reflect thoughts I've had about mistakes I made and experiences I've had (and am having) with my own three sons. (Two of them are recent college graduates, while the third is just now applying to colleges.)

Please spend some time reading this chapter. A few hours of your time invested in thinking about your career now will pay you back a thousandfold. That, I can promise you.

HOW TO PICK A GREAT CAREER

To get your thinking moving in the right direction, here are some tips about how to get a job you love. They are all based on my own experiences as an employee, employer, and independent consultant.

- The mere fact that you like computers (or books, horses, stamps, or whatever) doesn't mean you'll like making a living with them. There is a big difference between enjoying something as a pastime and enjoying it as a job. Often what initially seems fun and/or romantic about the subject disappears quickly when you make it your profession. This is true for a hundred different reasons. But they all add up to one thing: Just as it's impossible to know the secret of making any business successful by studying it from the outside, it's impossible to understand how any job feels without actually doing it. A prime example is acting It looks like the best job in the world, until you do it and realize you spend 11 hours a day waiting around for someone to call you to a scene and then listen to someone else yell at you for another hour or two.
- Instead of focusing on businesses or products that you like to use, focus on activities that you like to do. Are you a talker? A thinker? Do you like to write? When comparing one sort of job to the next, look at specific positions and find out what kinds of activities comprise most of the time spent.
- When approaching your job search, ask yourself what you want to get out of your career. Do you want to be wealthy? Do you want to bring about social change? Do you want weekends free to pursue a hobby? Do you

want summers free to go smoke jumping? When you discover what you want to take from your career, you will find that your options have narrowed considerably.

- Look for work that will make use of your unique talents. Your academic and extracurricular experiences will help you determine what your gifts are. Maybe your eye for great art means you'll have a talent for creating eye-catching brochures and reports. Maybe the accolades you won for your volunteer work mean you have a talent for working with other people. Your talents can translate into things you would not only excel at but enjoy doing long term.

- Ask yourself what type of environment you want to be part of. Do you resist a strict dress code? Do you enjoy the energy and pressure of deadlines? Do you work best when left to your own devices . . . or do you need strict parameters for each assignment? If, for instance, you enjoy sleeping late and hate stress, you may not be happy in an investment-banking firm. If, on the other hand, you love a creative and hands-on environment, you might be happiest working at a group-oriented marketing firm. You must consider not only the profession but also how that profession goes about conducting business.

- Although you will never truly know what a job is like until you've done it, researching those that sound interesting can help you decide whether you'd be a good fit for a certain position. Libraries and bookstores are full of books about varied career options. Not only will these books give you insight into the inner workings of specific professions. They can also provide you with valuable tips for pursuing a career in one of those fields.

- Ask people you trust about the jobs they've loved (and hated) the most. Your favorite uncle may share your passion for computers, so why not ask him if he's happy as a computer programmer? Your mother may share your gift for drawing, so why not ask her what she liked and disliked about working as an art director? Be sure to discuss a career with people who are certain to be honest about its benefits as well as its drawbacks.

- A great way to discover whether you'd be well-suited for a certain job is to accept an internship in that field. While you may not be doing the same type of work that you'd be doing as a full-time employee, you will be able to see the job from a new perspective. You may even be able to get hands-on experience. The law graduate who discovered she didn't like lawyers only *after* she joined a law firm could have saved herself a great deal of trouble by interning at the firm before she accepted the job. She might have been happier working at one of the many other jobs a lawyer can do.

- Once you have identified your passions as well as your talents, be sure to expand your job search to many types of careers. The mere fact that you love to write and have a talent for research doesn't mean your only possibility of happiness is in becoming a writer. You should explore a wide range of positions that involve both writing and research—grant writing, technical writing, journalism, and so on. Limiting yourself by determining that only one position is right for you could have disappointing results.

- In thinking about what kind of business you want to be in, you should consider not only your own talents and interests but also your hopes and expectations.

Specifically, you should spend some time answering the following questions:

1. "How long do I want to work?"
   a. "As long as possible (i.e., until I die)."
   b. "As short a time as possible (i.e., until I become financially independent)."
   c. Something in between?
2. "How hard do I want to work?"
   a. "I want to work hard forever."
   b. "I want to work hard now but take things easier later on."
3. "How much change do I need in my job to keep me interested?"
   a. "I can tolerate a good deal of routine."
   b. "I want as little routine as possible."
   c. "I like a healthy mix."
4. "How comfortable am I with personal interaction?"
   a. "I'm very comfortable with it."
   b. "I'm somewhat comfortable with it."
   c. "I prefer to work alone."
5. "How do I feel about being a boss?"
   a. "I like the idea of people working for me. The more people, the better."
   b. "I wouldn't like to have people under me. I'd rather go solo."
   c. "I could do it either way."
6. "How much wealth do I want to acquire?"
   a. "A low seven-figure number is fine with me."
   b. "Ten or twenty million would be better."
   c. "The truth? I want to be super-rich."

You don't need to arrive at definitive answers to all of these questions, but thinking about them should help you home in on the kind of working lifestyle that would be good for you—both now and later on, when you are older and ready for a different, more relaxed routine.

- Sometimes, discovering what it is that you *really* want to do comes down to good old-fashioned trial and error. Even if you accept a job, work hard, and give it plenty of time, you may end up feeling dissatisfied with your career. This is not the end of the world. Statistics indicate that most people will hold between 8 and 10 jobs in their lifetimes, which means that you might not find your ideal profession on the first try. So you reevaluate your passions and your talents, you do more research into careers that interest and excite you, and you find a different job.

Once you've considered all these possibilities, you will be well on your way to finding a great career.

THE FOUR TYPES OF BUSINESS

Here is something else that might help you decide on a career. It's a way of getting an inside feeling for any industry, even though you are standing on the outside.

My comments and conclusions in this section are generalizations, so they don't apply to every job and every person. Like most generalizations, they don't tell you what will always happen in the future. They can, however, give you a good idea of what probably will take place. In any case, they'll help you think about jobs and careers in a new way.

Whatever you intend to do for a living—whether it's selling

stocks or painting landscapes—it's a business. And all businesses fall into one of four categories:

1. Retail
2. Service
3. Wholesale
4. Manufacturing

Business and/or economic textbooks would call this an oversimplification. But for the purposes of our discussion about your future, it works well. It simplifies the world of working into four categories, each with its own pluses and minuses as far as your future happiness is concerned.

The Dope on Retail

Retail, for example, is usually the first thing most people think of when they think of business. They think of restaurants and supermarkets, bookstores and movie theaters. The retail business often seems fun and easy—and for that reason, it is very attractive. But the reality of working in the retail sector is usually very different.

There are several distinguishing features of retail that set it apart from the other business sectors in terms of how you might enjoy (or detest) the work experience:

- Generally speaking, the retail business requires you to be in one place for regular periods of time. It does not allow for a great deal of flexibility in terms of hours or travel. Being in the retail business in a serious way (serious enough to make a good living from it) means that you will be tethered to a ball and chain. The ball is the store. The chain is your obligation to keep it running properly. The most common problem retailers have is finding good people to sell the product and protect the merchandise. Finding, training, and managing retail workers is not something that can be done here and there on a hit-or-miss basis.

- The retail business is heavily dependent on location. If the city you are in decides to do six months' worth of roadwork right in front of your store, you may go bankrupt waiting for it to finish. Your customers can find somewhere else to go, but you can't. You're chained to that location. While this is going on, you still have to pay all your bills, including rent, utilities, and employee expenses. You can boost sales with good marketing and sales strategies in the retail business (just as you can with any business), but you can't work miracles. The lion's share of your success will depend on walk-by traffic.
- It's tough to get rich with retail. You can make a living—maybe even a good living—and you can enjoy yourself. But you can't get rich. The only retailers who are rich have thousands of retail operations. But they are not retailers themselves; they are marketers of retail operations. There is a big difference.

So if you (1) don't really like to spend time talking to people, (2) like to travel a lot, and (3) want to get super-rich, retail is probably a bad choice for a career.

What About the Service Industry?
This, too, is something that quickly comes to mind when we think about business. Maybe you can start a local lawn-care service. Or maybe you can hire a bunch of plumbers and have them work for you. How much you can make depends on what service you provide. But the services that seem the most

fun or glamorous usually pay the least. Why? Because of supply and demand: plenty of bright people vying for a limited number of good positions.

Service businesses include blue-collar hole digging, middle-level technical work, white-collar executive work, and, finally, the professions.

Yes, accountants and lawyers are service providers. So are plastic surgeons, speechwriters, and most entertainers. I include entertainers in this category because they share the essential characteristic of the service sector: At the end of the day, you are charging for your time. And if you want to make more money, there are only two ways to do it:

1. Charge more per hour.
2. Work more hours (though there are only so many hours you can work and still have a life).

If you ask most graduates what kind of work they want to do, the answer you'll probably hear most often is, "Something that involves working with people." And that's what is good about the service business. You will indeed spend most of your time interacting with people.

Much of that time will be a lot of fun, and your affability and social skills will come in handy. But some of that time will be stressful; some of it, downright disagreeable. No matter how much of a "people person" you may be, it's hard to enjoy yourself when you are being screamed at by some rich slob who isn't happy with the color of the trampoline your event-planning service provided for his five-year-old's birthday party.

The lower ranks of the service sector are replete with high-stress, low-pay jobs. As you climb up the ladder, the pay increases, but as a general rule, it is less than you'd get in manufacturing or wholesale.

The upper echelons of service work include professional jobs (doctoring, lawyering, accounting, and the like) and entertainment. Professionals, you may be surprised to know, don't make as much money as you'd think from watching television. Take a look, for example, at the median yearly income for the professions listed in Table 3.1.

Do you want to be a comedian? An actor? A writer? A filmmaker? Now you are really talking bad pay and crummy working conditions. The last time I checked, the average compensation for a professional writer in the United States was less than $5,000 a year. Acting? Not surprisingly, it averages close to what you'd get for waiting tables. (Why? Because that's how 90 percent of so-called professional actors pay the rent.)

TABLE 3.1

Income Levels by Profession

Profession	Median Yearly Income
Physician (urologist)	$259,294
Psychiatrist	$157,570
Physician (general st)	$144,623
Dentist	$116,026
Attorney	$107,666
Pharmacist	$94,054
Optometrist	$91,684
Research veterinarian	$81,842
Electrical engineer	$73,957
Civil engineer	$70,963
Staff nurse (RN)	$57,139
Architect	$46,851
Human resources generalist	$46,571
Accountant	$42,080
Insurance agent	$39,066

The travel and hotel industry is famous for demanding long, hard hours from its rank-and-file workers, and even more grueling time commitments from management. Pay levels are miserable, and benefits are next to nothing.

As you can see, I'm not too hot on service-sector jobs. It seems to me that they offer the patina of fun and/or glamour but deliver lots of stressful hours at relatively modest pay.

Now, Let's Say Something Good about the Service Industry

All that said, if I had nothing going for me today—no money, no education, and no connections—I'd probably start a service business. I'd cut lawns, install shutters, or fix roofs.

Why? Because the world is always in short supply of good service people.

Service is a great entry-level business opportunity for an ambitious new graduate, because it's an easy industry to get into. And starting a service business is a great way to learn a trade while earning money. If you make up your mind to do a great (not just good) job at a fair or cheaper-than-average rate, meet your deadlines, and keep your promises, you'll find yourself climbing to the top of the ladder in no time flat.

As your business grows, you can gradually increase your fees. If you work hard to find good workers and offer them the chance to develop in their own right, your business will grow. Eventually, you won't be doing any of the actual service work yourself . . . just developing new client relationships and renewing old ones.

This pattern isn't unique to the service industry. It's a blueprint for success no matter what you do. Start off by providing great service (or a great product) at a reasonable cost. As your business improves, you can raise your prices. As your prices increase, your clientele will become wealthier. A wealthier

SUCCESS THROUGH INVENTION

Imagine, if you will that it has been three years since you graduated from college. You are walking through the accessories department at Bloomingdale's—and something catches your eye. There, prominently displayed, is a product you designed. And you know that it is sold not only in Bloomingdale's, but also in Nordstrom, Neiman Marcus, Wal-Mart, and Target stores across the country!

That's the experience Melody Kulp has whenever she steps into one of the many department stores, salons, and boutiques that sell her distinctive Sparkles hair ornaments.

Sparkles evolved from an idea Melody had while hanging loose flowers in a friend's hair. When approached by a buyer from the exclusive Los Angeles store Fred Segal, she knew she had something special. Soon after Fred Segal began selling them, she had the pleasure of seeing celebrities such as Jennifer Aniston and Sarah Michelle Gellar wearing them.

Melody and friend David Reinstein—also 23 at the time—founded Mellies LLC in 1998. By 2000, Mellies Sparkles had produced nearly $9 million in sales.

Melody advises other entrepreneurs to push ahead even in the face of doubters. "There will always be people who say you can't do something or can't reach your goals," Melody said. She believes that staying focused and doing what you believe in are essential to success.

Sources: Debbie Selinsky, "Sparkle Plenty," *Success*, September 2000; "Young Millionaires," *Entrepreneur*, November 2000

clientele means more and better back-end sales opportunities. And that means a better and more financially rewarding life for you.

The problem with the service industry is related to its main advantage. It's so easy to get into that you will have lots of competition as your business grows. That means you'll be squeezed on your prices, making profits tough to get and salaries low. This is especially true of the glamour service industries, such as travel and anything to do with the media.

Then There's the Business of Wholesale . . .

Wholesale is a pretty good business, although it takes a while to develop. Today, the opportunities for wholesale are in China and Indonesia. Anything made in the United States can be made in those countries at a fraction of the cost.

But getting good, inexpensive products is only the beginning. The tough part of wholesale is developing a retail customer list. And, unfortunately, your customers will eventually figure out that they can probably cut you out and buy directly from the manufacturer.

The secret is to develop unique products that can't be duplicated. This you won't be able to do right off the bat—but over time, this is the way to go.

Some of the most popular wholesale products are the following:

Beauty supplies	Jewelry
Ceramics	Knives, tools, and personal security
Chemical cleaning compounds	Lumber and construction materials
Clothing	Machine parts and supplies
Commercial equipment	Men's and women's fragrances
Computer parts and supplies	Motor vehicle parts and supplies

Confections	Office supplies
Craft supplies	Paper and paper products
Electrical goods	Petroleum and petroleum products
Entertainment equipment	Plants and flowers
Furniture	Plumbing and heating equipment
Groceries	Professional equipment
Hardware	Scrapbooking products
Health and fitness products	Security electronics
Home and garden supplies	Stationery
Janitorial supplies	Wall coverings

Once you've developed your unique product, you'll need to sell it to retailers. This will involve going to trade shows, which can be expensive and time consuming. The top trade shows, for example, can cost thousands of dollars to attend. You will spend a lot of time talking with retailers and displaying your product, and you may end up with no cash—just a pile of orders to fill later.

Discouraging as it may seem, this is where you have the potential to make the big money. You could possibly take orders worth tens of thousands of dollars. (Remember, though, that you won't see the cash up front. You'll receive payment for those orders over a long period of time.)

By setting up specific payment policies, you may be able to gain some control over when you receive payment for your product. At his web site Guide to the Arts and Crafts Business, William T. Lasley ("Wholesale versus Consignment," September 2005, artsandcrafts.about.com) lists some payment terms you could use when dealing with your retail customers:

Policy #1: Customers must make prepaid payments. If you use this policy, you might want to offer a small discount in order to encourage your customers to pay up front.

Policy #2: Customers must make pro forma payments. This means that you will notify your customers when their orders are ready to ship. Each customer must then make payment before shipment.

Policy #3: Customers must make payment on delivery. This means that you'll receive payment as soon as your product arrives at the customer's door.

Or You Could Try Drop-shipping . . .

Because building a customer base is a difficult aspect of wholesale, you could try drop-shipping.

But My Favorite Type of Business . . .

My favorite type of business is what I'm calling "manufacturing." And in that general category, I include all sort of things that aren't normally considered manufacturing. I include, for example, publishing, as well as the selling of natural products, nutritional products, and the like. Manufacturing, to me, is any industry in which you create the product and sell it directly to the end user.

I love this type of business because it gives you complete control over the entire selling process, from inventing the product to closing the sale and even going back to the customer for more sales.

In the age of the Internet and globalization, manufacturing is a great business to be in. To create your product, you can use anyone the world over. And you can sell to the entire world, too.

So if you can't figure out what you want to do but want to get wealthy while you figure things out, get into a manufacturing business.

SOME POPULAR MANUFACTURING BUSINESSES

Artist supplies
Audiocassettes and CDs
Body-flattening products
Candles
Chocolates
Coffee
Collectibles and rare coins
Collectible toys
Consumer electronics
Cosmetics
Diet and weight-loss products
Do-it-yourself home decoration
Do-it-yourself home improvement
Do-it-yourself legal guides
E-mail publishing
Fashion accessories
Fishing equipment
Fitness and exercise videos
Fruit baskets
Gardening seeds and tools
Hobby and craft products
Home health tests
Jewelry and gems
Jogging supplies
Magic: tricks, instructions, and gag gifts
Mail-order books
Models: military

Models: nonmilitary
Natural health products
New-age products
Newsletters: business
Newsletters: financial
Newsletters: general
Newsletters: health care
Newsletters: travel
Pens
Pet supplies
Photography
Privacy products
Publishing
Real estate courses
Self-improvement programs
Sewing: patterns, notions, and accessories
Special reports
Sporting goods
Tobacco
Tools
Toys
T-shirts
Venture capital financing
Videos
Vitamins and nutritional supplements

Now that you are more aware of how to go about finding the right career, you're probably wondering how you can possibly compete with all the other new graduates to actually *get the job*. As you'll discover in Chapter 4, getting the job involves much more than sending out stacks of resumes.

CHAPTER 4

YOUR NEXT AND BEST-EVER JOB

As a recent college graduate, you may be feeling tremendous pressure to find a job—any job. But accepting the first job that comes along will get you nowhere. Getting the right job now matters—not only for your wealth but also for your health and happiness.

Here's what you don't want: to spend the next several years struggling with a job that doesn't motivate you, pays you poorly, and doesn't advance your career. If you do that, you'll almost certainly find yourself having to start over just to get headed in the right direction.

In Chapter 3, I explained how to pick a career that will both satisfy your intellectual and emotional needs and allow you to become wealthy at the same time. In this chapter, we will cover the next critical step: getting a good job in the field of work you have selected.

MOST OF WHAT YOU'VE BEEN TOLD ABOUT JOB HUNTING IS WRONG

Most people end up with a job as the result of a combination of loosely structured plans, half-baked notions, unsure actions, and/or fortuitous occurrences. If you ask a dozen executives to retrace their careers you'll probably hear a dozen versions of "this happened" and "that happened" but very few stories that sound like "I wanted this, so I did that."

I've read many books about job hunting. Most of them were full of bad advice. What they explained (sometimes well, sometimes poorly) was how to do well *what everyone else is already doing.* When you are competing with hundreds of qualified people for one good job, doing what everyone else is doing—even if you do it especially well—won't get you the job. Why? Because the person to whom you are sending your resume is getting dozens or even hundreds *just like yours!* When writing resumes, most people do exactly the same things. They emphasize their strengths, hide their weaknesses, and make identical claims:

- "I am highly organized."
- "I get along well with people."
- "I'm a natural leader."
- "I am a self-starter."
- "If I have one fault, it's that I can't tolerate bad work."

Maybe you are highly organized. Perhaps you are a natural-born leader. But when everybody else applying for the job is making the same claim, what's a human resources manager going to do? He or she will have no way of knowing that your claim is the one true claim in the bunch, so the manager will discount it along with all the others. Your resume will be given the once-over, and if there is any evidence of imperfection—a mispunctuated sentence, a reference to a hobby the manager doesn't like—it will be tossed in the trash basket. How do I know? Because I've deep-sixed thousands of conventional resumes.

Human resource people are tired of sorting through the same old cover letters and reading the same old curricula vitae. And they are fed up with hearing the same old lines. If you really want to get hired, you have to distinguish yourself. The best way to do that is to forget about the standard resume and cover-letter package altogether and replace it with a more sophisticated, more personalized pitch that is based on proven direct-marketing principles.

Direct marketing is the science of creating positive responses (sales) with letters. As a young person seeking your first career-oriented job, you are likewise going to be seeking positive responses with letters. By using the secrets of the direct-mail industry, you'll dramatically increase your chances of getting the kind of response ("Come in for an interview!") you are looking for.

The best book I've read on this subject is Jeffrey Fox's *Don't Send a Resume* (Hyperion, 2001). Fox compares the job hunt not to direct marketing per se but to something similar: direct sales. He says that sending conventional resumes to potential employers is the equivalent of a salesperson's making a cold call:

> Cold calls have a low success rate. The customer may have absolutely no need for the product, may not even be in the office. . . . The person who receives the resume may have no need for an additional employee, may not even be the hiring person (p. 5).

Fox is right. The reasons the conventional approach to getting a job hardly ever works are that standard resumes and cover letters are too broadly written ("Dear Sir" or "To

71

Whom It May Concern"), they are sent out to too wide an audience, and they talk too much about the sender and too little about the reader. Anybody who's been in the sales or direct-marketing business for even a few weeks will tell you that these are three major strikes against you.

THE FIRST AND MOST IMPORTANT
SECRET TO FINDING A JOB

The most important thing you need to realize about getting a job is this: The people who will be reading your letter are *not really interested in you.* They have not been hanging around all their lives waiting for you to finish college and write them a letter. In fact, they're probably very busy and may be annoyed that they have to read your letter in the first place. The moment they get the feeling that you are just another kid out of college blanketing the industry for a job, they'll toss your letter into the wastebasket.

If they're not interested in you, then what are they interested in?

I'll tell you: They're interested in *themselves.* And if one of them is the right boss for you, that person is also interested in his or her business—the problems and the challenges he or she faces every day. This employer may be in need of an assistant, but he or she doesn't care about how wonderful that person is. This boss just wants to know one thing: "Can this person solve my problems?"

To be specific, employers don't care about your career goals, what you like to do in your spare time, and what organizations you've joined. They are used to seeing that kind of information on resumes, and they may even ask you questions about some of those facts during an interview. But they're doing so only because they're hoping to discover something more important about you. And that is some version of the answer to "Can this person solve my problems?"

THINK OF GETTING THE PERFECT JOB
AS A DIRECT-MARKETING CHALLENGE

Let's talk about direct marketing some more. In a conventional direct-marketing situation, a businessman writes a letter selling one of his products. If he knows what he's doing, he will make that sales letter very specific and personalized. Though he is sending the same letter to a group of people, he will address each one of his prospects by her name and make her feel as if he is writing to her and her alone.

He'll also let her know right away that he understands her problem (maybe a health problem, a beauty problem, or a business problem)—and he'll claim to have a solution to it. Finally, he will show the prospect all the many ways that her life will improve once she has bought and used his product.

The direct marketer knows that, to make a sale, he can't waste his prospect's time by talking about himself. Everything he writes must be focused on the prospect's problem and how much better her life will be after she's bought the product.

This is exactly what you have to do when you send out job-hunting letters. You have to let your prospective employers know that you understand exactly what their problems are and that you have solutions for each and every one of them. You have to be correct in identifying their problems and must be convincing in arguing that you have the solutions for them.

Think of it this way. When seeking a job, you need to remember the following:

- The letter and the resume are parts of a direct-mail promotion.

73

- The letter is intended to sell. As a sales letter, it must be about the customer's problems—not your strengths, weaknesses, or wishes.
- The customer is the person you are going to work for.
- You are the product—the product that is going to solve that person's problems.

It's very important that you send your letter directly to your prospect—the person you are going to work for—not some stooge in the human resources department. You must do everything you can to find out who your prospective boss is and get your letter into his or her hands.

Once you've done that, you need to sell your "customer" on the idea that you can make his or her life much easier and the business much better if you are hired. You can't just say it; you have to convince the boss of it. To do that, you need to figure out specific ways you can save the business time, hassle, and waste, and ultimately boost sales and improve profits.

But how do you find out all this stuff about the company or companies that you want to work for?

Start with the industry.

LEARN ABOUT THE INDUSTRY AND COMPANY YOU WANT TO WORK FOR

The way to land a great job is to narrow your field. Choose an industry. Pick the top 50 businesses in that industry. If possible, give preference to those businesses that are growing. You have a much better chance of getting a job and moving up in your career by getting involved with a growing company.

Out of the 50, target a limited number of potential future employers—three or four. Then make it your goal to learn everything you can about each business. Research the company's history, its practices, and its products. Research its competitors and identify in each case the differences between them. Read all the press releases and annual reports available for each business. Determine its goals, problems, and challenges. While you're at it, find out the secret to the company's growth.

Here is the absolute minimum information you should know about a potential employer:

- The company's annual sales (approximately)
- Its primary profit center (what really makes its money)
- Its greatest business strength
- Its greatest business weakness

You won't get this information from a brochure. You'll have to make a few phone calls and/or read some reports. Get in touch with employees, competitors, and/or industry analysts—and ask questions.

Find out what it takes to excel at the job you want. Look into what your prospective employer looks for when hiring entry-level people. And figure out the tricks and skills the successful people in that field use to get to the top and stay there.

Now you understand the important facts about the industry, and you have learned something about how your target company works—specifically, how the department that might be hiring you works. But you need to learn how to get your cover letter to that all-important person: your prospective boss.

LEARN ABOUT YOUR FUTURE BOSS

After you've looked into the business itself, find out whom you want to work for—the exact person. This may take more research, but it is important to address your resumes and cover letters to real people rather than to nameless human resources representatives. Figure out what that person needs to make his or her own life better. Does he or she need someone who can improve the company's products? Reduce costs? Increase sales? Reduce the time wasted in following up on things? Find out what it is that your prospective boss needs, even if you have to do so by having an informal "informational interview" with the person (more about how to do this later). Another good way to determine what an employer needs is to get firsthand knowledge of what his or her business is lacking. To do this, you can get a job with the company as an intern.

Once you know everything possible about your prospective employer, write your sales letter to that person. The letter should state, respectfully and concisely, how you intend to help achieve the employer's objectives if you are hired. Remember, you are selling yourself. So treat this as an opportunity to sell your future boss on your product: you. Be specific. Make strong promises. Your letter can be a formal letter, a personal note, an interoffice memo, or even an e-mail. The medium you use is a matter of what's appropriate for the relationship. But the fundamental nature of the letter remains the same.

ANATOMY OF A GREAT JOB APPLICATION LETTER

A great job application letter should do the following things:

- It should say something good about the company and the person you want to work for.
- It should let your prospect know that you know his or her goals, problems, objectives, and so on.
- It should make the claim that you are the person to solve/achieve them.

- It should prove that you are that person.
- It should make a specific request (ask for the job).

It's okay to send a resume along with your sales letter. It should serve as a quick-reference guide to your previous successes and strengths instead of giving a lot of superfluous information about hobbies or career objectives.

If you write a great letter, you'll no doubt get a chance to prove to your prospective employer, face to face, that you're the right choice for the job. When you get the interview, show him or her that you are determined to work day and night to prove that you are the best employee he or she has ever hired.

Remember, this employer wants you just as much as you want him or her. All employers hope to find superstars to make their lives easier and their businesses more successful. As a future superstar, you are going to fill that role for your employer.

Do all the other, less important things, too—such as dressing properly and giving the employer a good handshake. But never lose sight of the main idea: You are the product. And you are the salesperson, too. Sell your prospective employer on what he or she wants to be sold on: that you will improve his or her life.

Once you understand the basic idea of how a good sales letter works—and realize that getting a job is selling yourself—it will become immediately apparent that 95 percent of the resume writers out there are doing it wrong.

That, of course, means more opportunity for you.

HOW TO LAND THE JOB INTERVIEW OF YOUR CHOICE

Here are eight direct-marketing techniques that you can use to dramatically increase your chances of landing the job interview of your dreams:

HOW TO BE BRILLIANT IN A JOB INTERVIEW
WITHOUT TALKING (MUCH)

Jeffrey Fox tells the following story in his book *Don't Send a Resume* (p. 114):

> Douglas MacArthur, the legendary World War II Army general, was looking to hire a new aide. After a staff review of candidates, MacArthur interviewed the short list. One of the potential aides was a young lieutenant. At the beginning of the interview, the general asked the lieutenant, "Did you have any trouble finding the place?"
>
> "No, sir," answered the lieutenant, who then asked, "Sir, what is your view of the role of the Army in winning the war here in the Pacific?"
>
> For one hour, interrupted only by the lieutenant's occasional "uh-huh" and "Could you elaborate?" the great general talked. At the end of the "interview," the lieutenant was offered the job. Later, MacArthur told one of his colonels that the young lieutenant was one of the most intelligent officers he had ever met.

I had a similar experience in graduate school when I met a visiting scholar. I spent 10 or 15 minutes telling him how much I liked his books and what an important critic he was and asking him fan-club-type questions. He later said to the department chairman, "That young man is extremely bright. He's one of your best students, in my view." He formed that opinion without knowing a single thing about me or what I could do, and without hearing a single opinion of mine . . . except how much I admired him.

This is important to remember when you are seeking a job. It's useful in any interview, but especially so if you get to talk to the person you'll be working for.

1. The envelope you send should be of good quality, and the address should be typed in a way that makes the letter look personal. It should be addressed to a specific person: Mr. Daniel James, Vice President of Marketing. This should be the person you want to work for. Never send resumes out addressed to generic titles (Personnel Manager, Accounting Manager, etc.), and never use bulk mail. And don't allow your post office to meter your mail. The more your envelope looks like something that might have come from a friend, the greater the chances that it will get opened.

2. Your cover letter should be very personal. As we discussed earlier, it should indicate that you (a) know the company in some detail, (b) like the company, and (c) believe you have something specific and valuable to contribute to it.

3. If you include a resume, it should be specifically tailored to the individual company you are applying to. Each resume should be a carefully crafted and unique piece.

4. Don't use self-serving clichés (such as "a passion for helping people") that virtually any job candidate can make. Instead, use facts, incidents, and numbers to reveal your qualities and capabilities.

5. When writing about your accomplishments, focus on what you have done recently (say, in the last few years).

6. If you have no relevant experience, don't try to pretend you do by making a job at Burger King sound like rocket science. Here is where you make up for your lack of experience by showing specific knowledge of the company and industry you aim to work for. If you've done your homework well, you will be seen as a blank slate with great potential (always desirable).

7. Don't summarize your career, experience, or skills at the end of the letter. State the facts briefly and clearly—once.

8. Remember the value of having connections. Each company wants to know as much about a potential employee as possible in order to make the right decision about who to hire. So do what you can to be recommended by someone in the company you want to work for—or by someone in the same industry. By eliminating one more "unknown" from your background, you'll have an advantage in getting an interview. Most hiring managers work with their peers at other companies when looking for employees, and many candidates are hired through such referrals. So never stop networking. And if you have a contact inside your target company, make sure you mention him or her in your letter!

While you are putting in the good stuff, make sure you don't include any bad stuff.

HOW TO RUIN A GOOD RESUME

Most career counselors and employment experts would agree that people tend to make the same mistakes when writing their resumes. These mistakes include:

- *Lack of focus.* Like any headline, a career objective must grab the reader's attention. If your resume is vague, pretentious, or rambling ("A challenging, rewarding position that will enable me to get to the highest pinnacle possible with my experience"), you risk losing the reader.
- *Inaccurate or false information.* Because many companies

check your education and job references, you risk your career by padding your resume with half-truths or lies.

- *Listing references* There's no need to list references—it's understood that you'll provide them when asked.
- *Unclear writing.* Don't worry about complete sentences, but do make sure to convey your points clearly.
- *Salary requirements.* Your current or desired compensation is an issue you can raise during your interview.
- *Gaps in your employment history.* It's not a good idea to exclude any job you've held—even if it ended badly. Find another way to solve the problem, short of fudging. Consider using years only, instead of months and years (1996–1998 versus May 1996–June 1998).
- *Typos.* Proofread your resume and ask a friend or family member to proofread it as well. Even one spelling error could land your resume in the trash.
- *Including unnecessary information.* There's no need to include your age, your marital status, your reason for leaving your current job, or a physical description of yourself.
- *Excluding critical information.* Your resume should clearly state your name, address, phone number, and e-mail address.

Using these dos and don'ts as a guide, you will be able to write a clean, informative resume that is specifically targeted at your prospective employer.

BEFORE THE INTERVIEW: ASK FOR AN INFORMATIONAL INTERVIEW

Targeting your best prospects and sending them tailored resumes and cover letters should get you plenty of interviews.

But what do you do if your heart is set on one particular company and that company doesn't invite you in?

Here's a clever technique that could work. Call the office of your prospective boss and ask for a short, nonthreatening *informational interview.* An informational interview is a great way to get in that locked door and find out a lot of personal and professional information about your target prospect.

A properly conducted informational interview will tell you exactly what promises you should make later on, when you do get that job interview. And once you've actually met and listened to the boss talk about himself or herself for 20 or 30 minutes, your chances of getting a job interview are—needless to say—now much better. If you do a really good job at the informational interview, you may even end up with the job you want before you leave the office.

Here's a quick example:

Phone call, Monday afternoon: "Thank you for taking my call, Mr. Jones. As your secretary probably told you, I'm just out of college and want to work in your industry. I've been watching your career, Mr. Jones, and have admired what you've done. I specifically liked that last marketing campaign you did for Camel cigarettes. That was a very clever campaign. I was wondering, Mr. Jones, if you could spare me 10 or 15 minutes one day to ask you about your career so I can be better prepared to succeed in this industry when it's time to get my first job."

Informational interview, Thursday morning: "Thank you so much for seeing me. I know you are very busy. I won't be more than 10 minutes. My, what an impressive office you have! Tell me, Mr. Jones, what would you say is the most important thing a young person like me would need to learn to be successful in your business?"

Half an hour later: " Well, the truth is, I'm ready to start working now. Really? You'd be interested in hiring someone like me? Gee. I don't know what to say. I'm flabbergasted. I'll tell you this: I will never disappoint you. I'll work day and night. I'll follow every suggestion. I'll listen to every word you say." (And so on.)

Monday morning: You've got the job.

Once you're an employee, you have to make good on your promise to never disappoint your boss. When you get to Chapter 5 of this book, I'll give you lots of suggestions about how to make yourself invaluable to your organization.

BEFORE THE INTERVIEW: FIVE THINGS TO DO

Your interview should be approached with the same amount of seriousness as your resume and cover letter. So before the interview, take the time to plan out what you're going to do and say.

- If you have any control over the situation, try to interview after all other candidates have finished. Hiring consultants say that the last person interviewed has a slight edge over previous interviewees—and having any edge over the competition can never hurt.
- Be prepared to tell your interviewer exactly why he or she should hire you. This is a chance for you to put your research to the test. Show that you know the company well enough to know exactly how you can be an asset. Explain just how you will make your boss's life easier by being his or her employee.

- Know your strengths and weaknesses—as they are relevant to this job. Honesty is important, but it is probably a good idea to withhold the information that you burst into hysterical tears right before a deadline. Instead, focus on weaknesses that you have overcome.
- Have a list of your future goals. Your interviewer may want to know where you see yourself in 3 years, 5 years, or 10 years. Make sure your goals are ambitious but realistic. An interviewer may be put off if you say you see yourself as CEO in three years. The interviewer may be equally put off if you mention that you see yourself in the same position indefinitely.
- Refresh your memory about your extracurricular activities. Interviewers often ask about one's hobbies and pastimes. According to an article in *USA Today* ("Common Interview Questions," in the "Careers and Workplace" column, January 29, 2001), interviewers are not simply curious as to whether you have a life—they are probably looking for evidence that you have job-related skills outside of your professional experience. If, for example, you play chess or bridge, that shows you have analytical skills. Reading, music, and painting demonstrate your creativity. Individual sports show that you have determination and stamina. And participation in group sports indicates that you are comfortable working as part of a team.

AT THE INTERVIEW: SEVEN SALES TECHNIQUES THAT WILL LAND YOU THE JOB

Once you get that interview, don't waste the good work you've done so far by coming in and doing what most everyone else does.

What do most people do? I'll tell you.

They come in (dressed in their best suits), sit down, and try to smile. They answer the first few questions nervously, and then, as time goes on, they relax and start talking about themselves. The more questions they are asked, the better they like it.

By the end of a half hour, they've spent 20 minutes talking about all the ways they think they are wonderful and every hobby they enjoy doing. If they are lucky, they've devoted five minutes to a discussion of the job they will be doing—and in that time, they might have said something like "I'm sure I can do the job."

This kind of interview is not going to get you the job. It's at least safe to say that if it does, it is only because the other interviewees were even lamer than you were.

You don't want to be hired because you were the best of a bad lot. You want to set a fire in your future boss's imagination. You want to get that boss thinking about how much better life will be the moment you start working for the company. In the words of Jeffrey Fox (*Don't Send a Resume,* p. 89): "If you don't know why the company should hire you, it's a good bet the company won't know either."

Here are some specific sales techniques you should use when you go for an interview:

- Have a specific objective in mind and work hard to achieve it. If you haven't been promised it by the end of the interview, ask for it (nicely).
- Remember that the hiring interview is a sales call. Let the customer talk as much as he or she wants. Listen. Nod your head. Smile and agree. When the interviewer asks a question, give the answer that he or she wants to

hear. If you have been listening closely, you will know what that is.

- Consider showing something—a customer survey, industry data, or the like—that illustrates the work you've already done and helps make the case that you can contribute to the company's success. The tactic of showing is a time-honored staple in the repertoire of strong salespeople.
- If you interview at a restaurant, don't drink alcohol and/or order something and eat very little of it.
- In your research, discover dress preferences, if any, of the company you're interviewing for. Don't be a rebel. Conform.
- Don't try to befriend your prospective employer.
- If you feel you might not get the job you are seeking, suggest that you can do a project for the company on a freelance basis. Perhaps even free. "That way, you can find out if I can do what I've promised," you can say, "without any risk on your part." This works in selling vacuum cleaners. It should work when you're selling yourself.

AFTER THE INTERVIEW: THE ALL-IMPORTANT FOLLOW-UP

Once the interview is over, write a thank-you note. You don't have to write pages and pages—just a few lines to thank the interviewer for taking the time to speak with you.

A thank-you note has three purposes. It reminds your prospective employer of your interview. It gives you a chance to restate your most persuasive argument for why you deserve

GOOD MANNERS AND SUCCESS

Despite what some pundits have said, making people like you is not the secret to success. In fact, there may be an inverse relationship between affability and accomplishment. If you spend too much time and energy trying to please others, you won't get your own work done.

There is, however, no reason for arrogance and no possible excuse for rudeness. With a little extra care and attention, you can attain everything you want in life—reach all your goals and accomplish all your objectives—without making people dislike you. How do you get what you want without offending others? The answer is simple: with good manners.

Being well-mannered means acknowledging people each time you meet them, remembering their names and something about them, expressing yourself in a thoughtful manner, and saying "please" and "thank you."

It's surprisingly easy to forget your manners as you climb the ladder of success. With each step up in power and prestige, it's easier to ignore a courtesy or to take one without thanks. If you don't watch yourself you can turn into someone you wouldn't like.

Here's a quick checkup on your manners:

- Do you smile and say "hello" to everyone you meet each day?
- Do you listen attentively when others speak?
- Do you refrain from raising your voice or losing your temper?
- Do you say "thank you" every time it's warranted?
- Do you criticize people carefully and in private?
- Do you praise people specifically and in public?
- Are you mindful of your appearance?
- Do you know the first and last names of all those who work with you?

ENTREPRENEURIAL SPIRIT

Mix Jergens, cocoa butter, baby powder, and Neutrogena together in a big bottle and you have a business. At least that's what six-year-old Farrah Gray thought when he decided to sell his homemade lotion door-to-door in his Chicago housing project.

That initial venture made a mere $10 in profits—but his foray into the world of food made him a teenage millionaire. After developing his grandmother's homemade syrup into a strawberry-vanilla flavored concoction, he launched Farr-Out Foods—and the company hit sales of $1.5 million the year Gray turned 14.

Gray began with a dream and fueled that dream with "sheer determination." In a January 2005 television interview with Tavis Smiley, he said that you have to stick to what you know and "find your area of excellence." To discover what it is that you excel at, ask yourself three questions: "What comes easy to me, but harder to others? What would I do for years and years to come and never have to get paid for it? How can I be of service?" Gray also advises young entrepreneurs to never fear rejection, to seize every opportunity, to network with everyone you meet, and to see each success and failure as a learning experience.

Now 20, Gray runs *InnerCity* magazine, invests in real estate, and makes speeches. He has also written a book, *Reallionaire: Nine Steps to Becoming Rich from the Inside Out* (HCI, 2005). His plans for the future include hosting his own talk show and perhaps even running for president.

Source: "Getting Rich from the Inside Out," *PR Newswire,* January 10, 2005.

the job. And it proves that you not only have good manners but also care about the job.

A good thank-you note has the following characteristics:

- It is on stationery, not scrap paper.
- It's handwritten, not typewritten.
- It mentions the prospective employer by name.
- It says something specific about the interview.
- It includes the words "thank you."

Writing a thank-you note is an extremely simple task. But, simple as it is, most people don't remember to send one. You should do it immediately after any sort of interview, informational or formal. The fact that you took the time to thank your potential employer for meeting with you will set you apart from the other applicants.

A WORD ABOUT PERSISTENCE

It should be clear from everything I've said so far that persistence is essential if you're going to succeed in this world.

That shouldn't surprise you. Of all the qualities that contribute to an accomplished life, none is more important than persistence. Intelligence, knowledge, connections, luck—they are all important ingredients in the stew of success, but persistence is the stock.

Here's a little story about persistence—or the lack thereof: A few years ago, I attended a conference in Florida where about 200 would-be copywriters had assembled to learn more about the direct-mail business and make contacts. J.T., the publisher of a large direct-mail company, invited the crowd to contact her if they wanted to try out for freelance positions.

Shockingly, only 8 of the 200 came up to her after her speech and signed up for the opportunity. Imagine that—192 out of 200 were too busy, scared, lazy, or whatever to take advantage of the kind of career opportunity that comes only once or twice in a lifetime. The eight who did respond were asked to send J.T. writing samples. Only one person did! Keep this story in mind the next time you feel like you are competing against too many other people.

CHAPTER 5

HOW EASY IT CAN
BE TO EARN A VERY
HIGH INCOME

Regardless of what work you are currently doing—whether you've landed your dream job or are flipping burgers to pay the rent—the work habits you develop now can make a huge difference in the amount of wealth you eventually acquire.

In this chapter, we are going to take a look at how some workers—a select few—skyrocket to the top of their fields and enjoy the benefits of achievement: better career options, more favorable networking opportunities, more helpful mentors, and a higher income. Specifically, I will show you how to elevate your income to six figures in five years or less.

The advice I'm giving you is based mostly on my personal experience and the experience of about a half dozen protégés of mine who have done just that. For example:

- R.J.'s income went from $29,500 a year in 1996 to $50,000 in 1997 and then $215,000 in 2000. Since then, it has never dipped below $200,000.
- L.H. was making about $60,000 in 2002. Today, he's earning more than $250,000.
- F.N. has had a similar experience, seeing his personal compensation rise from $31,000 in 1998 to $159,000 in 2001 and to more than $400,000 today. (I heard from a mutual friend yesterday that he expects a seven-figure income this year.)
- J.B. enjoyed a skyrocketing salary increase from about $60,000 a dozen years ago to more than $500,000 today.
- T.W. was making less than $20,000 when I met him. Today, less than 10 years later, he's making more than a million.

HOW I BOOSTED MY ANNUAL INCOME FROM $14,000 TO MORE THAN A MILLION DOLLARS

Before I got married, I was an average worker—by which I mean that I showed up. Woody Allen has famously said that 80 percent of success is just showing up. I know what he means. He's talking about an aspect of extraordinary success that often involves being in the right place at the right time. But his maxim doesn't apply to becoming a great employee and earning an extraordinary salary. For that, you're going to have to do more than just show up.

My years of *just showing up* provided me with lots of experience, jumping from one interesting job to another, but it never got me a very high income. In fact, I don't think I got a single decent raise until I was married and realized I had to do more than just get to work and do my job.

To become wealthy in 40 years, you don't need to earn an above-average income. All you need to do is save 15 percent of what you make and wait. But we've already agreed that there is no good reason to wait 40 years to enjoy the benefits of financial independence. If you follow the recommendations in this book, you'll be wealthy much faster—even in as little as 7 to 15 years.

To achieve that kind of accelerated wealth, you need to start by boosting your income. It stands to reason, I think you'd agree, that to get a better-than-average salary you have to be willing to do a better-than-average job. If you put into action the recommendations I'm going to make in this chapter, your income will increase substantially in the next few years. If you can boost your income by, say, $50,000 to $100,000 in the next five years yet maintain the same expenses you have now, that will be a whole lot more money you'll be able to invest in your future.

In addition to the extra income you'll enjoy, the techniques you learn in this chapter will help you achieve all your objectives in life—even those that have nothing to do with money.

IT TOOK ME A WHILE TO FIGURE OUT
HOW TO BOOST MY INCOME

After I was married and had a child, I got serious about work and started getting good raises. My starting salary at that time, as an editor with a Washington, D.C.–based newsletter-publishing company, was $14,000 a year. Four years later, I was earning $30,000. That's an increase of about 21 percent a year.

Making a 21 percent increase every year will get you very rich over time. But when you are starting off in a career and moving up, the increases you get tend to be considerably higher than what you get later. Given the business and industry I worked for then, I could have expected my income to double again in the next 10 years. (That's assuming I continued to be an above-average employee.) An increase from $30,000 to $60,000 in 10 years represents a yearly rate of 7 percent. That's not bad, but I wanted more.

A year later, in 1982, I decided to get rich—and within a year after making that decision, I was making $150,000. Two years later (maybe sooner, I can't remember), my income was in excess of $1 million. I was earning more than a million dollars a year, back in the early 1980s, and I was still an employee!

Looking back on that experience, I see that my income "acceleration," as it were, occurred in two phases. The first phase was in transforming myself from an ordinary to an *extraordinary* worker. The second phase was in moving up from extraordinary to *invaluable.*

By the way, please excuse my use of the adjectives *extraordinary* and *invaluable.* I know they sound bombastic, especially since I'm talking about myself. I'm using those words because they convey something important in their literal meanings:

- An ordinary worker works the way most workers do.
- An extraordinary worker does substantially more than the average worker.
- An invaluable worker makes such a significant contribution to the company that losing him or her would be considered a major financial misfortune.

Let's get back to my story and see how these stages of work performance affected my ability to demand a higher salary.

PHASE I: BECOMING AN EXTRAORDINARY EMPLOYEE

In 1982, as I said, I was working as the editor of a couple of newsletters (one about Latin American politics and another about African business and economics) for a small, Washington, D.C.–based publishing company. I was earning $14,000 a year, and my wife was earning less than that. Our two salaries could barely cover our ordinary living expenses. On top of that, I was attending graduate school and we were paying off student loans. Then our first son was born. For the first six months of his life, he slept in an open drawer in our bedroom.

Recognizing that I had to take the monetary side of my work more seriously (up till that point, I was concerned mostly with trying to become a famous writer), I knew I had to change the way my boss, Michael, and his boss, Leo, felt about me.

Until then, they saw me as a bright kid who was on the borderline of being more trouble than I was worth. I got to work and did my thing, but I had the typical young writer's hatred for everything that had to do with the business side of business.

I didn't like marketing, and I loathed sales. I didn't even like to include renewal forms in the envelopes that carried our newsletters. I would be perfectly happy to try to make the editorial content of the newsletters better—if Michael were to ask me to do that—but he would be wasting his time if he thought I was going to help him with a sales letter.

That prejudice against business had to change, I realized, if I expected to get an above-average raise.

My target was to get a $2,000 raise. If I didn't change my work habits, I knew, my raise would probably be about $500. So I decided to win over Michael and Leo.

I began by working longer hours and doing everything Michael asked—immediately and well. He remarked on the improvement in my productivity. Within a month, he was favoring me over the other employees, ever so slightly, when it came time to delegating responsibilities.

Knowing that Leo was very concerned with expenses, I spent a week looking into ways we could reduce them. Although we were a small organization, we spent a good deal on typesetting and printing. By calling around town to typeset shops and printers, I was able to come up with a plan to reduce our yearly costs by about $48,000.

I presented my plan to Michael by way of an interoffice memo, copied to Leo. Even though he had nothing to do with my cost-cutting idea, I was careful to give Michael partial credit for it. To win Leo's attention, I wasn't going to risk losing Michael's approval.

Leo boosted my income to $16,000 several weeks later. That was my goal, and it represented, I realize now, a 14 percent increase. That was about five times the company's average and probably more than I deserved. But I think both Leo and Michael were so impressed with my transformation from an average, semitalented, reluctant-to-help writer to a helpful member of the business team that they wanted to reward me.

I was happy with my raise but at the same time realized that unless I continued to improve, my next raise wouldn't be as big. I'd get a better-than-average increase, because I had turned into a better-than-average employee, but that wouldn't satisfy me.

To get more, I knew I had to give more. So, without being asked, I redoubled my efforts to keep expenses down and worked to improve the editorial quality of our newsletters. As a result of my efforts, the newsletter renewal rates improved. This brought in more revenues and higher profits.

Over a period of three years, I came up with dozens of ideas that reduced costs and improved the quality of our products. By my coming in early, working late, and being the go-to guy when problems arose, my salary increased from $16,000 to $30,000.

That was a 23 percent yearly increase. Thirty thousand dollars doesn't sound like a lot today. (You will earn that or more starting out.) Back then, however, it was substantial, especially when one considers my industry and the business I worked for.

In my first three years of paying attention to my job, I learned one very important secret about making a lot of money as an employee:

- To earn significantly higher raises than the average person, you must perform at a significantly higher level than your coworkers. So long as your work performance is ordinary, you can't expect anything more than an ordinary salary. But if you change your work habits and contribute substantially more than your fellow workers, you can rightly expect to be paid substantially more than they are getting.

PHASE II: BECOMING AN INVALUABLE EMPLOYEE

In 1982, I moved to Florida to take a position as editorial director of a bigger newsletter-publishing company that had set up shop in Boca Raton. I applied my newfound work ethic to my job as editorial director—with a vengeance.

My starting salary—at $35,000—was already an improvement. But by applying what I'd learned to this bigger, faster-growing company, I was able to bring about bigger improvements. Instead of boosting renewal income by $50,000 a year, I could make a $500,000 difference.

The same ideas. The same amount of work. But applied to a larger, faster-growing company. That was a second important secret I discovered about making a great income as an employee:

- It's not just *what* you do at work that matters but with *whom* you do it. To get the maximum value out of the hard, smart work you do, be sure that you are working for a boss who's willing to promote you and also for a company that is growing (so that there will be better positions waiting for you).

This is a wealth-building secret you shouldn't gloss over. In assessing the job you are shooting for, give serious consideration to the person you'll be reporting to, the part of the business you'll be working in, and the business itself.

- What you want in a boss is a smart, experienced person who is going places.
- The things you want in a department or division are growth and an orientation toward sales.
- What you want in a company is a potential for significant growth.
- What you want in an industry is also growth potential.

If you have a choice—and you will if you follow the advice in Chapters 3 and 4—you should opt for a smaller, faster-growing company over a larger, staid business. The larger business will give you more perks and the appearance of more stability, but the smaller, faster-growing company will give you a much greater chance to boost your income.

Remember—there are three factors in getting rich: how much you invest, how long you invest it, and over what length of time you invest it. How much you save is a function of how much you make. The faster you can boost your income into the $150,000-plus category, the faster you'll be able to start saving significant chunks of money each year. That's why we are putting so much stress on income.

My decision to become rich had an extraordinarily powerful effect on everything I did thereafter. Before then, the business problems I faced often seemed confusing. If, for example, I was faced with the recommendation that we improve the quality of the paper stock of our books and newsletters, I wouldn't be sure exactly how to respond. Yes, a better quality of paper would improve the look. However, it would cost more. What to do? Given the new perspective I'd acquired by committing to getting wealthy, I had a simple way of thinking it through: How much would it cost—and how would that equate to any possible improvement in sales? If the cost exceeded the perceived financial benefits, my inclination would be against spending.

Before deciding to get rich, I was confused by a host of interests that were antithetical to building the business and making profits. I was interested, for example, in winning industry awards and developing prestige in the marketplace. Since neither of these goals had any discernible benefit in terms of making the business grow, I now saw them as inappropriate personal indulgences.

When you put your business before yourself, problems that once seemed foggy clear up quickly. Challenges that once seemed important drop suddenly to the bottom of the priority list, and other objectives rise up.

In a matter of weeks, I reorganized my staff (fired someone who was holding me back and hired a superstar who worked for a vendor), changed our product line (got rid of a favorite publication that never made any money), and streamlined the marketing department to make it easier and faster to launch new promotions.

Because of the work I did, my boss, J.S.N., offered me an increase of $20,000—to $55,000. Although $20,000 was one of the biggest raises he'd ever given (and the biggest I'd ever received), I wasn't satisfied. I asked for more.

"I really appreciate the raise," I told him. "But I've decided to become rich. And to hit the target I've set for myself, I need to make $70,000 this year, not $55,000."

For a long moment he said nothing. Then he leaned over and looked me in the eye: "But you're not worth $70,000," he said.

Having anticipated that "welcome back to reality," I was prepared with an answer: "I know I'm not worth that kind of money," I admitted. "But if you'll invest in me now, I will make it up to you a hundred times later on."

J.S.N. was (and is) one of the best negotiators I've ever known. If he wanted to, he could have dismantled me at that point. But there was something about the earnestness of my plea and the confidence of my conviction that won him over.

He thought about it overnight, and the next day he called me into his office and told me not only that he would give me the $70,000 but that he hoped to someday make me into a millionaire.

I had done something that day that was much more important than I realized at the time. I had successfully negotiated a huge increase with an exacting boss—and had also gotten myself a world-class mentor. J.S.N. was someone who could, and did, teach me how to get rich. He'd gotten rich three times over in his past careers. The newsletter-publishing business was going to be the fourth one.

And J.S.N. had done himself a favor that day, too. In letting me know that he believed in me and intended to help me, he won the lifetime loyalty of a young man who could—and did—help his business go from just a million dollars in sales that year to more than a hundred million.

THE THIRD GREAT DISCOVERY ABOUT
EARNING A HIGH INCOME

In an effort to achieve a dramatically higher personal income, I had transformed myself from an average worker to an extraordinary worker. And by deciding to become rich, I had taken my transformation one step further: I had become—to the business—almost invaluable.

Let's reiterate.

To get your income into the $150,000-plus range in five years or less, you need to do three things:

1. You must develop the working habits of an extraordinary worker.
2. You must attach yourself to a fast-growing company.
3. You must become an invaluable employee of that company.

ORDINARY PAY RAISES WILL MAKE YOU
POORER, NOT RICHER

Most people go through their lives working for businesses they care nothing much about, dealing with problems they'd rather not face, and getting paid wages they'd very much like to change.

In the past 35 years, the average wage increase in the United States has been about 5.8 percent. During that same period of time, inflation has averaged 4.8 percent per annum. That means the average worker got a real annual wage increase of only 1 percent. As you can imagine, you can't get rich if your buying power (which is what income after inflation amounts to) increases only 1 percent a year.

A NEW APPROACH TO AN EXISTING BUSINESS

Most 16-year-old boys have little to zero interest in the business of flowers. Jonathan Barouch, however, was not like most 16-year-old boys. After an embarrassing experience at a florist shop, Barouch decided there had to be a better—and less humiliating—way to buy flowers. His online company is now one of the top three florists in Australia and New Zealand, generating more than $1 million in revenue.

Barouch founded FastFlowers.com.au in 1999, while still in high school. In the early days, the company struggled to compete with local florists. He also faced obstacles in the form of investors who were skeptical of his youth. But Barouch persevered. "It was a bit disheartening, but we didn't give up," he told Joanna Tovia of *Finance News* in an interview.

His persistence and tenacity have paid off. FastFlowers has developed relationships with several larger corporations, including Qantas Visa, Westpac, Telstra Big Pond, Bendigo Bank, and American Express. The company delivers flowers to every city in Australia and every country in the world. "It went from a joke bedroom business into a business that's kept me busy for six years," Barouch told Tovia. And the company continues to expand. It has recently begun to offer fruit baskets and gift hampers along with floral arrangements.

Sources: Joanna Tovia, "Online Flowers Blooming Fast," *Daily Telegraph,* January 25, 2005; "Young Entrepreneur's Blooming Business," www.breadtv.com.au, posted July 14, 2005.

But here's the good news. You don't have to worry about net-income increases of only 1 percent a year if you follow the recommendations in this chapter. Your income will increase in two ways: You will outpace the average salary for your position because you will work harder than your fellow employees. And you will outpace the usual career advancement curve (i.e., you'll be promoted higher and faster) because you will have skills and knowledge that will make you special.

In the following tables, I'm going to show you what you can expect to make by earning an income that is higher than the average. The first column in Table 5.1, at 1 percent, indicates how your real income (net income after taxes) would grow over a 40-year period in today's terms, net of inflation. The figure at the bottom of that column represents approximately how much you'd be making—in today's dollars—at the end of a 40-year career. As you can see, at $44,720.45, it's not very impressive.

TABLE 5.1

Estimated Income with Different Levels of Salary Increase

Ordinary		Extraordinary		Invaluable	
1% SALARY INCREASE		5% SALARY INCREASE		10% SALARY INCREASE	
Year	Salary	Year	Salary	Year	Salary
1	$30,337.00	1	$30,337.00	1	$30,337.00
5	$31,568.80	5	$36,874.81	5	$44,416.40
10	$33,179.13	10	$47,062.64	10	$71,533.06
15	$34,871.60	15	$60,065.18	15	$115,204.71
20	$36,650.40	20	$76,660.09	20	$185,538.33
25	$38,519.94	25	$97,839.86	25	$298,811.34
30	$40,484.84	30	$124,871.21	30	$481,238.65
35	$42,549.98	35	$159,370.82	35	$775,039.66
40	$44,720.45	40	$203,402.04	40	$1,248,209.12

The next column, at 5 percent, indicates what I believe you could easily get (again, on a net basis after inflation) if you become an extraordinary worker. At the end of 40 years, working at that level, you should be earning an income that is about five times higher than you would by being ordinary.

And the third column, at 10 percent, represents how your income would grow (again, on a net, time-adjusted basis) if you become an *invaluable* employee. In this case, your income would be about 30 times as high as you'd get by being ordinary. When it comes to earning an income, "just showing up" just doesn't cut it.

So you should now realize the following things:

- If you are satisfied being an ordinary employee, you will never earn enough money to grow wealthy.
- If you contribute significantly more to your business than your fellow workers do, you can expect to see significant pay increases over time. These increases will be enough to give you a better lifestyle, but they will make you wealthy only after many, many years of scrimping and saving.
- It is only by making yourself an invaluable employee that you can expect your income to skyrocket.

Keep in mind that there is nothing in Table 5.1 that allows for the compounding benefit of working for a great boss in a strong division of a fast-growing company. Nor does this table take into account what can happen if you make the transition to being an invaluable employee early in your career.

That's the Automatic Wealth strategy: to dramatically boost your salary by dramatically boosting your value—and fast. If your salary were to hit the $150,000 mark in five years or less, Table 5.2 is what your lifetime income would look like.

Table 5.2 shows you how your income could increase if you got really high salary increases for five years and then enjoyed 10 percent annual increases thereafter. In 40 years you'd be making more than $4 million.

It's unrealistic to think that you could make that kind of money—unless, of course, you became CEO of a very profitable company. But if you did make yourself invaluable to your employer and if the business you worked for was growing and profitable, it's perfectly reasonable to think that your compensation could rise from $30,000 to $150,000 in five years and then from $150,000 to about a quarter of a million dollars thereafter.

I have worked with dozens of young executives that have enjoyed that kind of income appreciation and a handful who were making between $500,000 and $2 million a year in 10 years.

If you want to get an idea about how much money you can make at the business you are working for now (or plan to work

TABLE 5.2

Estimated Future Salary Income (with 10% annual increase)	
Year	
1	$30,337.00
5	$150,000.00
10	$241,576.50
15	$389,061.37
20	$626,587.23
25	$1,009,124.99
30	$1,625,205.89
35	$2,617,410.34
40	$4,215,365.53

for in the future) find out how much the senior executives are making now. Ask yourself if that's enough to meet your standards. If so, then you are in good shape. The only thing you have to worry about is getting from the mailroom to the boardroom in a time frame that meets your needs.

If you want to dramatically increase your personal income, you must dramatically increase your corporate value. And that means transforming yourself from an ordinary employee to an extraordinary employee and then from an extraordinary employee to an invaluable one.

But what are the specific steps you need to take to make that transition?

HOW TO BE AN EXTRAORDINARY EMPLOYEE

If you want an extraordinary income, you have to transform yourself into an extraordinary worker. Here are five ways to do that:

1. *Get in early.* There is no better way to demonstrate your commitment to your company than by getting to work earlier than everybody else. Getting to work early sends a good message: "I'm here! I am eager to work! I'm ahead of the crowd!"

2. *Understand your responsibilities.* You may have received a job description when you were hired, and it may do a pretty good job of telling you what you have to do. But until you understand how what you do affects your boss's bottom line, you'll never be able to make good decisions about which projects to focus on. The best way to do that is to make an appointment with your boss and ask, "What are the top 10 ways I can make you more successful at your job?"

Don't worry about appearing to want to curry favor with your boss. Tell your boss you realize your chances of success depend on his or her success. Say, for example, "I'm not asking for specific to-dos. Once I know your main objectives, I will be able to make good decisions on my own. That's why I'm asking. Because I want to make sure my work plan is in gear with yours."

3. *Focus on what's important.* Once you know what your boss needs from you, apply Pareto's Law to your work. Pareto's Law says that 80 percent of the success of just about anything comes from 20 percent of the attention it's given. So list your boss's top 10 priorities. Then identify the 2 that will have the greatest impact on his or her success. (Hint: They will probably have something to do with improving the company's bottom line.) Those are the priorities that you will focus on. (Keep in mind that your boss may not know what his or her priorities should be. After working with your boss for a while, you may have a better idea of what will contribute to his or her success than he or she does.)

4. *Never say no.* Employees often wonder whether saying yes to every request will make them look weak or dependent. The answer: no. Your boss *wants* a yes to every request he or she makes of you. Saying no—though sometimes warranted—may sound like you are moving against him or her. If you have already established your work priorities by taking steps 1, 2, and 3, you'll have no problem identifying requests that don't contribute to your boss's (and your) success. When asked to do something of that nature, tell your boss that you will be happy to get to it at some time in the future, but at the moment you are working on things

that you believe he or she would rather see done. Then list what those things are. Chances are, the boss will modify or even drop the request. If not, you can be sure there is a good reason why.

5. *Improve your skills.* Unless you keep growing—in terms of your knowledge and skills—you can't expect your income to keep rising. Ask questions about every aspect of your business that is related to what you do. Find out what you can about the other areas—especially sales and marketing. Read executive memos. Take work-related courses. Have regular chats about business with the power people in your business. Implement what you learn in your work.

6. *Communicate your progress.* Doing your job well is good. And getting better at it as time passes is better. But unless you let your boss and other powerful people at work know about your progress, you can't be sure they will help you. Make it a habit to update your superiors, in writing, on the challenges you face and the objectives you've achieved. In promoting yourself professionally, follow these three rules:

- Tell the truth. False promotion is worse than none at all.
- Be generous with credit to others.
- When reporting your accomplishments, be specific . . . and keep your ego in check.

HOW HARD DO YOU HAVE TO WORK?

Developing these five work habits isn't easy. You may be thinking, "I'm not sure I want to work that hard." If so, consider

oyees work to simply *get by*. Some actually try ork as they can get away with. Even employees uctive often waste much of their time doing k like writing long memos about issues that o the business . . . or arguing points that don't much matter . . . or working on projects that don't really affect the company's bottom line.

In most businesses—which likely includes the company you get your first good job with—only a very few people get in early and stay focused on what really matters.

In my reading on the topic, many employment experts explain that workers fall somewhere on a bell-shaped curve when it comes to diligence and follow-through. At the bottom of the curve are the loafers and goof-offs. In the middle is the silent majority that does just enough to get by. At the top are the relative few who are motivated to achieve.

When you understand the dynamics of any such group, you understand that a modest amount of hard work will put you beyond both the terminally slothful and the lump-along middle crowd. Just by being modestly ambitious, you will rise to the top third of almost any organization. But getting up the last few rungs of that ladder—into that top 20 percent—will be tough, because the few you are competing against are competing hard. Chances are, they are as smart and talented as you, with the same (or more) basic resources. They may even have better contacts. But there is one thing they don't have more of, and that is time.

If you can use your time more effectively than they use theirs, you will move ahead of them. Hard workers eventually succeed even against those who have advantages. You can do better than someone who is smarter, richer, and luckier than you—so long as you are willing to work harder than that person does.

People who rise to the top work long hours, but not excessively long. They are at their desks early—at least an hour before

HOW TO GET PROMOTED

If you practice the five work habits described in this chapter, you will easily rise to the top 20 percent of your company's workforce. Extraordinary employees get extraordinary raises—but how do you speed up the process?

Remember, when you get recommended for a promotion, your superiors are betting their reputations on you. To make them take that risk, you need to do more than just do a good job. You need to do three more things.

1. *Stand out from the crowd.* Make sure you have a broad range of competencies and abilities in many areas. It's great to have strengths, but if you have only one area of expertise, you run the risk of being cast in the same role again and again. You want your employer to recognize your potential to perform well at a variety of tasks.

2. *Get to know people outside your department.* Turn every possible opportunity—whether it's a holiday party, your lunch break, or a meeting—into a chance to meet someone new inside your company. Develop a friendly rapport and establish yourself as reliable and competent.

   Once you've made contact with someone new, ask him to introduce you to his coworkers or even his boss. This network of corporate contacts—including colleagues, subordinates, and superiors—can help you when you need a new challenge or want a promotion.

3. *Plan for every possible outcome.* While you may not be able to anticipate *every* possible outcome, you should have a game plan in place for several different

scenarios. Think through what you would do in a given situation, how you would react if a meeting went badly or if a sale fell through. Your ability to change directions when you meet an obstacle will show your employer just how adaptable you are.

To these recommendations, I would add the following: You should try—to whatever extent possible—to demonstrate the skills of the job you are seeking as soon as you realize you want it. There's no better way to show your capabilities than by starting to do the relevant tasks before the job opens up.

First, volunteer to help the current jobholder. A job worth having is usually complex and demanding. That means the person whose job you want will probably feel—sometimes, at least—swamped. How could this person resist your pleasant proposition to do the chores he or she doesn't have time for?

Remember, the most important factor in getting ahead is to gain the trust of the people you work with—your subordinates, your colleagues, and your superiors. And you can't possibly get their confidence unless you merit it.

I am talking about respecting the fundamental unwritten rule of hierarchy: "If you support my position, and you prove yourself to be superior, when it is time for me to move upstairs, I'll recommend you to replace me . . . but only if I can trust you to continue to support me."

When it comes to self-preservation, people are at their smartest. They listen with their full attention. They watch what you do. They overhear what you say to others.

So be careful. And make up your mind that you will have integrity.

others—and they stay later (though it may be only a half hour later). But what they do best is work smarter when they work.

They do the necessary things first, even if they are difficult. They learn what they need to know and don't waste business time learning unimportant stuff. They are willing to harass and cajole, tease and criticize, flatter and pout to get the job done.

They spend a few minutes every morning organizing their days and a little while every Monday morning planning their week. They select their tasks based on what will achieve their goals, not on what happens to end up in their in-boxes. They manage their jobs; they don't let their jobs manage them.

Hard work is by definition hard, but it's not all that hard if you know why you're doing it.

THE NEXT STEP: FROM EXTRAORDINARY TO INVALUABLE

By working harder and smarter to accomplish more, and letting key people know what you are accomplishing, you'll find it pretty easy to get above-average raises. But how do you earn those really high incomes? I'm talking about $150,000 to $500,000 or more?

The answer, as I've indicated before, is twofold:

Step one: Learn (and eventually master) a financially valued skill.

Step two: Apply that skill to your company's core profit-generating activities.

Good employees earn good salaries because they are valued personnel. But great employees earn amazing salaries because they are considered *invaluable* to the company. To be truly invaluable, you have to be, more or less, irreplaceable. The closer you can get to seeming to be irreplaceable, the better your chances of radically increasing your income.

The most important thing you'll need to do is this: Master a financially valued skill.

STEP ONE: LEARNING A FINANCIALLY VALUED SKILL

A financially valued skill is one that plenty of other people are willing to pay you good money for. How good? Let's use the number we've been shooting for: $150,000 per year.

This is, admittedly, a somewhat arbitrary number. But it does have the advantage of giving you an after-tax income of about $100,000. That's enough for you to enjoy a reasonably comfortable lifestyle *and* put at least $22,500 into savings.

By working harder than your fellow employees, you can expect to see your income grow by about 10 percent a year for the next five years. That would get you up to about $50,000. But is $50,000 enough to grow rich on?

No, I don't think so. And neither do you. What we want to happen is this: for you to keep your expenses in check with an income that appreciates to $50,000 over five years, while your actual income shoots up to $150,000. If you can do that, you'll be able to save not just 15 percent of $50,000 (or $7,500) but 25 percent of $100,000 ($25,000).

That's a big difference. Do you want to know how big?

Let's look at the first year's savings; if you invest $7,500 over 40 years at 12 percent, you'll have about $340,000. If you invest $25,000 over the same period of time at the same rate, you'll end up with $1,132,000.

And remember, that's just your first year's savings. Imagine how that would add up over a career!

Okay, so what specific skills are going to command that kind of salary increase? What are the skills that typically get that kind of money in the workforce?

How to Be a Top Earner in Your Business

There are three basic kinds of jobs in the business world: administrative, technical, and profit-generating.

- *Administrative jobs* include most positions in corporate management, product fulfillment, operations, and customer service, as well as some positions in finance and accounting.
- *Technical jobs* include most positions in information technology and engineering and some positions in the legal, financial, and accounting fields.
- *Profit-generating jobs* are those that are directly involved in producing profits for the company. Profit generators include marketers, salespeople, copywriters, people who create new products, and the people who manage all of these employees. In most companies, the leading profit generator is, of course, the CEO, because the CEO's main job is to deliver a bottom line.

Administrative workers, on the average, constitute the poorest-paid group. Generalists by training, they compete against a large pool of other generalists in jobs that require no special skills or talents. If you are an administrator, and a very good one, you can expect to see your income rise as your performance improves. But more likely than not, it will be at the 4 percent or 6 percent level—probably not enough to meet your wealth-building goals.

Figure 5.1 shows examples of what you would earn working

Figure 5.1   Salaries for administrative jobs.

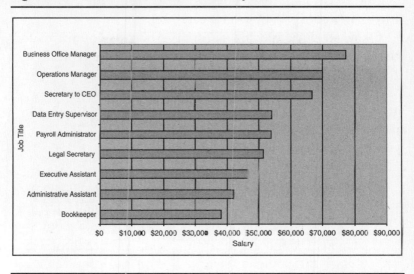

in different administrative jobs. Note: These salaries represent the amount earned by those who are in the top 25 percent of all workers in that field.

Technical workers are usually better paid than their administrative counterparts. This is especially true at the beginning of their careers, when even an entry-level position requires a high degree of specialized knowledge. Computer engineers, information technology people, and certified public accountants typically start at higher salaries than do fulfillment managers and customer service clerks—but the difference tends to diminish over time. Top engineers often make more than operational vice presidents, but not much more.

Figure 5.2 shows examples of what you would earn working in different technical jobs. Note: These salaries represent the amount earned by those who are in the top 25 percent of all workers in that field.

115

Figure 5.2   Salaries for technical jobs.

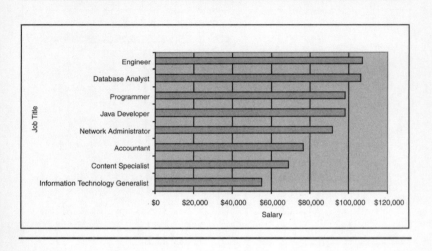

Profit generators are usually the highest-paid employees. More important, they have the greatest potential for income growth.

Figure 5.3 shows examples of what you would earn working in different profit-generating jobs. Note: These salaries represent the amount earned by those who are in the top 25 percent of all workers in that field.

As you can see by comparing Figures 5.1 through 5.3, profit-generating jobs claim a significantly higher salary than technical and administrative positions. While the highest-paid administrator listed in Figure 5.1 earned less than $80,000 a year, the lowest-paid profit generator listed in Figure 5.3 earned over $100,000.

There is another basic category of jobs that is a cross between technical and profit-generating: professional jobs. These are the jobs that require specialized knowledge and education.

Figure 5.4 shows examples of what you would earn working

Figure 5.3   Salaries for profit-generating jobs.

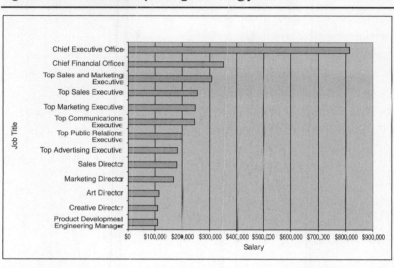

Figure 5.4   Salaries for professional jobs.

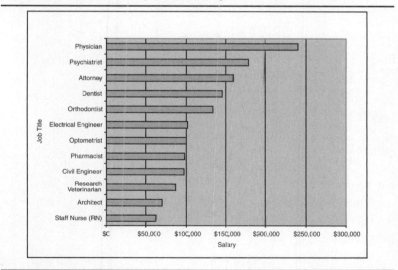

in different professional jobs. Note: These salaries represent the amount earned by those who are in the top 25 percent of all workers in that field.

As you can see from Figure 5.4, even people with specialized professional jobs don't earn the salaries that profit generators do. What does all this information tell you? If you want to be earning $150,000 or more, you need to get yourself a financially valued skill and put yourself into a profit-generating profession.

STEP TWO: APPLYING YOUR SKILL TO THE COMPANY'S PROFIT STREAM

Here's a way to think about getting above-average raises. I call it the 10-for-1 rule.

If you want to get a raise that's $1,000 more than ordinary, make sure you've been a major contributor to an idea that will generate at least $10,000 in additional net profits for your company. So if you want to increase your current income by, say, $25,000, you are going to have to find a way to increase business profits by about a quarter of a million dollars. And that's not just $250,000 once. It's $250,000 this year and next year and every year thereafter that you expect to maintain that much-higher-than-average salary.

In general, you'll have the best chance of having that kind of impact on your company's bottom line if you are working in one of several key, profit-generating areas:

- Sales
- Marketing
- Product creation
- Profit management

Yes, some engineers, attorneys, and corporate administrators earn $150,000 or more. But in companies where such functionaries earn big money, the marketers, salespeople, and profit-center managers are earning $250,000 to $500,000— sometimes more!

I'm not saying you should abandon your métier if you've been trained as a computer analyst, engineer, or accountant. I'm just saying that if you want to make a superhigh income, you have to become a supersignificant contributor to your company's bottom line. And that means you have to become an influential force in product creation, marketing, sales, or profit management.

Here's how you start:

- First, figure out how your business creates profits.
- Then, figure out how your job contributes to that process.
- Next, modify your job so that more profits are produced as a result of what you do.
- Finally, make sure that the people who are in charge of giving raises know how much more money you are making for the company.

How much do you know about your company's core profit strategies? Answer these questions:

- Can you name five *primary* benefits of your company's top-selling product/service?
- Can you name the chief *secondary* (psychological) benefit of this product/service?
- Can you name one *unique selling proposition* (USP) for each of your company's top-selling products/ services?

MAKE YOURSELF INTO A MARKETING GENIUS

Skilled marketers are consistently among the highest-paid individuals in any industry. They earn high salaries, extraordinary bonuses, and the respect and admiration of colleagues and competitors. Marketers who master their trades are all but guaranteed a life of wealth, security, respect, and satisfaction.

The best marketers know how to apply three fundamental principles.

The First Principle: The Difference between Wants and Needs
In today's consumer-driven economy, it's easy to mistake a want for a need. When you realize that your customers don't need your product or service, you recognize that the way to convince them to buy it is to stimulate their desire for it. The most effective way to do that in your advertising is to do the following things:

- Promise your prospective customer (usually implicitly) that taking a certain action (buying your product) will result in the satisfaction of a desire (want).
- Create a picture in your prospect's mind of the way he or she will feel when that desire is satisfied.
- Make specific claims about the benefits of your product and then prove those claims to your prospect.
- Equate the feeling your prospect desires (the satisfaction of a want) with the purchase of your product.

The Second Principle: The Difference between Features and Benefits
A pencil has certain features:

- It is made of wood.
- It has a specific diameter.

- It contains a lead-composite filler of a certain type.
- It usually has an eraser at the end.

These features describe the objective qualities of the pencil. So if buying were a rational process, selling would be a matter of identifying the features of your product.

But, as you just learned, buying is an emotional process. And that means you must express the features of your product in some way that will stimulate desire. You do that by converting features into benefits. For example, the features just listed might be converted into the following benefits:

- It is easy to sharpen.
- It is comfortable to hold.
- It creates an impressive line.
- It makes correcting easy.

The Third Principle. The Difference between Benefits and Deeper Benefits

The reason some marketers do a better job than others is that they understand the difference between benefits and deeper benefits.

In our example, for instance, what might be the deeper benefit of having a pencil that sharpens easily? To figure that out, master marketers ask themselves these questions: "Who are my target customers? And why, exactly, do they want little things (like sharpening pencils) to be easy?"

Of course, there's no single answer to such a question. It depends entirely on who those target customers are. If they're busy executives, their deeper reasons are going to be different than if they're busy housewives.

Master marketers who understand these deeper motives can create stronger advertising copy, because they will be appealing to emotions that are closer to their customers' core desires.

- What is your company's primary competitive advantage?
- How is that advantage employed in (1) product creation, (2) marketing, and (3) sales?

If you know your business the way you should, you will have quick and confident answers to all of these questions. If they leave you guessing, you have work to do.

Ask yourself this: "In the eyes of upper management people, is the work I do considered (1) nice but unnecessary, (2) necessary but not of much interest to them, or (3) essential to the growth and profitability of the business?" Income producers are viewed as not just "good" but "necessary" and "desirable." By making yourself one of the few people in your company who know how to bring in the bacon, you give yourself the greatest chance of getting big raises, big promotions—and eventually, a six-figure income.

MODIFYING YOUR JOB TO BECOME A CRITICAL FACTOR

If you are not currently (or haven't been trained to be) a salesperson, marketer, product creator, or profit manager, don't despair. You can keep your official job and still make the transition over to the money side of your business. The objective is to start making significant contributions to the bottom line and let the bosses know that's what you are doing.

Here's how to do that: Ask yourself which people in your company make the most money. Identify at least three distinct jobs. Now ask yourself which of those jobs you would most like to do.

It may seem like a stretch at the moment, but it's entirely possible that you could do that job. So, starting today, learn something about it. Find out what it takes in terms of hours and days. Find out what it typically pays and when it pays more and why. Ask about the daily routine, the common problems, the biggest challenges, and the best rewards. Ask. Observe. Read.

Keep it up, day after day, until you start to feel as if you understand the job. When you feel ready, talk to your boss about your plans. Then approach key people in the department you're interested in. Tell them (honestly) that you think their field is something you'd be good at. Say you've been learning about it in your free time and you'd like to volunteer to help them out whenever you can so you can learn even more.

People will be impressed by your willingness to dive in and give them a hand. If your intentions are sincere and your follow-up is diligent, you'll soon enjoy a reputation for being an up-and-comer.

NOT SURE WHICH SKILL TO MASTER? TRY THIS ONE

Of all the skills you can have—the ability to speak like Winston Churchill, the skill to paint like Rembrandt, whatever it takes to calculate like Albert Einstein—none will help you achieve wealth as well as knowing how to sell things.

So if you're not sure which financially valued skill to target, I recommend becoming an expert in the kind of sales that make your company profitable.

Every private enterprise functions the same way. To keep doing what it wants to do (and to make a profit from it), it has to (1) attract customers at a reasonable cost and (2) convert them into repeat buyers.

Every successful business is based on understanding the correct answers to two very simple questions:

1. What is the most cost-effective way of attracting customers?
2. What is the best way to keep those customers buying?

If you can learn to see your business that way and can one day discover the correct answer to those two questions, you will quickly become recognized as an invaluable employee. That will happen because you will understand your business from the inside out.

WHERE TO GO TO LEARN FINANCIALLY VALUED SKILLS

There are many ways to learn financially valued skills. You can learn pretty much everything there is to know about sales and marketing, for example, by reading these books:

- *Scientific Advertising,* by Claude Hopkins (Chelsea House, 1980)
- *Ogilvy on Advertising,* by David Ogilvy (Crown, 1983)
- *Tested Advertising Methods,* by John Caples (5th edition, Prentice-Hall, 1997)
- *The Copywriter's Handbook,* by Bob Bly (Owl Books, 1990)
- *Influence: The Psychology of Persuasion,* by Dr. Robert Cialdini (Perennial Currents, 1998)
- *The Tipping Point,* by Malcolm Gladwell (Little, Brown, 2000)
- *Selling the Invisible,* by Harry Beckwith (Oxmoor House, 2000)

CHAPTER 6

STARTING
YOUR OWN
MULTIMILLION-
DOLLAR BUSINESS

Starting your own business may be the furthest thing from your mind. You've just finished four years of study, are busy finding and starting a new job, and have an active social life. Why would you complicate everything by thinking about your own business? Here are the reasons, in brief:

- Control
- Money
- Self-satisfaction

You can enjoy these benefits as a salaried employee, but not usually to the same degree. I've been both an employee and a business owner—many times over—and can tell you from my own experience that nothing beats doing it yourself.

But that doesn't mean you should abandon your plans for

getting a good job now. Nor does it mean that you *have to* start your own business in the future.

The main purpose of this chapter is to get you interested in how businesses are built and developed. The knowledge you'll get from learning that will benefit you in a dozen positive ways throughout your career, even if you work as a professional, as a freelancer, or in a corporate environment.

For now, as a recent graduate, you should get yourself a good job. Working as an employee for someone else gives you all sorts of advantages you couldn't have if you were on your own, such as getting an inside view of worlds you may want to conquer, developing useful contacts, and getting mentored. Not to mention a steady paycheck.

The strategy I'd recommend at this point in your life consists of the following steps:

- Get a good job now.
- While you are turning yourself into an invaluable employee, learn something about small businesses and how they operate.
- Explore different businesses. Think about what specific kind of business you might want to run. Pay attention to the field you are in. Look for what's not working well or what could be done better. Talk to people. Read books. Consider whether the ideas you come up with would be expensive to develop or could be done in smaller increments, perhaps on the Internet.

If you do those things, your head will be full of exciting business concepts. At the same time, you'll have developed a good understanding of what it feels like to work for someone else. You'll be in the perfect position to make a decision to go out on your own, stick with what you are doing, or possibly do both.

It's always the third option (doing both) that I recommend. I call it the path of the "chicken entrepreneur." I favor that approach because (1) it's the road I traveled, (2) it's what has worked for my protégés, and (3) it affords a safety net—both for you and for your boss—if things don't work out. Although the ideas we'll cover toward the end of this chapter will give you the greatest protection against failure, it's important to realize that most new businesses fail. Your first business may fail, too, so you don't want to quit your day job until your side business not only gets a good start, but really takes off.

I've had the good fortune to start dozens of successful small businesses over the years. Most of them became multimillion-dollar enterprises. A few got much, much larger. That sort of track record is likely to give you a positive attitude. And I believe my optimism is valid. My evidence is the tens of thousands of other entrepreneurs who successfully launch businesses every year. Again, as I've said, many people fail in business, but many more succeed. If you subtract the foolish failures—restaurants being the most foolish, followed by any sort of glamour business (think travel, bed-and-breakfasts, sports, or the like)—the successes far outweigh the failures.

When I think about my own experience and the experiences of people I've coached and reflect on the larger numbers of successful ventures, it doesn't seem to me that starting a small business is all that risky.

You can reduce the risk of starting your own small business by sticking closely to what you already know. By "what you already know," I mean (1) the product or service you are going to sell and (2) the primary method by which you are going to sell it. Of course, as a recent graduate, you might know very little, if anything at all. Don't worry. You have the benefit of time—and time is all you need to build up your knowledge about any business.

DEVELOP AN AREA OF EXPERTISE

When you find an industry or business that you like—one that interests you—spend your first several years as an employee getting to know everything about it. This might sound daunting, but you are already familiar with the strategies. In Chapter 5, we discussed what you need to do to become an above-average employee. We talked about how to develop successful work habits and how to become part of the top 20 percent in your company.

These skills will not only help you increase your income but also give you the knowledge—in fact, the expertise—you need to start your own business.

Think of your employment as a free scholarship in the school of successful entrepreneurship. By spending focused time working to be a great employee, you'll learn lessons about business that you can use for the rest of your career. You'll find that your working experience will have taught you many things about what can make a business run more smoothly, how it can generate greater profits, and how some aspect of it can relate to another business.

BABY STEPS LEAD TO SUCCESS

By learning on the job, you'll develop many ideas for starting your own businesses. Some of these ideas will be small, specific ideas or techniques that you will know exactly how to implement. Other ideas will be bigger, broader, and perhaps more exciting.

When it comes time to try out these ideas on your new business, take baby steps—one at a time. By that I mean that you should be willing to try something new—but just a little

CHOOSE THE RIGHT ENVIRONMENT
FOR YOUR SMALL BUSINESS

In terms of lifestyle, peace of mind, and even accumulation of wealth, the "where" of your life is a very, very important decision.

Now is the best time to figure out what kind of physical environment makes you feel best. Not just every once in a while, but day in and day out. Once you know that, you need to consider, realistically, if you can run your dream business (or enjoy your dream profession) in a place that offers that kind of environment. I believe the answer is probably going to be yes. Advances in transportation and communication now make it possible to live almost anywhere.

What I've found is this: You should, if you can, (1) live in a physical environment that inspires you, and (2) work within walking distance of your home. These two factors have a huge impact on the day-to-day quality of your life. They affect, for example, how you feel when you get to the office, what you do on your lunch breaks, and how much time you spend and waste.

If you decide to ignore my advice and locate your new business where the best economics are, consider these *Inc.* magazine recommendations:

- The best big metro areas are Phoenix, Salt Lake City, Raleigh-Durham, Indianapolis, Washington (D.C.), Memphis, Orlando, Dallas–Fort Worth, and Nashville.
- The best small metro areas are Las Vegas, Austin, Fargo-Moorhead, Savannah, Sioux Falls, Jacksonville, Reno, Wilmington (North Carolina), Montgomery, and Tucson.

new. If, for example, you've learned how to sell cat food via banner ads on the Internet, you might consider setting up a business that sells cat food via small ads in magazines. (That's one baby step away from what you already know how to do.) But you shouldn't let yourself get into a business that sells cat health products through direct mail—even if you could convince yourself that you're an expert in selling cat products. Selling cat health products through direct mail is simply too many steps away from your core competence.

A typical start-up business based on something you know will break even or lose a little money in year one, make a decent "salary" for the owner in year two, and provide a substantial bonus—in addition to a good, arm's-length management salary—in year three. After that, it's usually straight uphill.

You can invest a small amount of money (and a lot of hard work and well-spent time) in a small business and see it grow into a business that is worth a million in seven years.

HOW TO MAKE THE TRANSITION TO YOUR OWN BUSINESS, ETHICALLY AND EFFECTIVELY

If you decide that you want to go out on your own, consider the following:

- Before you become a valuable employee, you will spend months and sometimes years producing so-so work. During that time, your employer pays your salary, provides for your benefits, and teaches you skills, industry practices, and company secrets.
- In return for investing so much in you, your employer expects you to be reasonably loyal. Usually, that means

sticking around and working hard after you've become good at what you've been trained to do.

- If you quit before you've had a chance to pay back your employer, you are cheating. And if you quit to start a business that was made possible by the knowledge you gained and the contacts you made as an employee—you are cheating your employer twice.

There is an ethical way to move from being a well-paid employee who is learning the secrets of a business to being an independent entrepreneur working on your own. Here it is:

- Be the best employee you can be. So long as you are employed, use everything you learn to help the company grow and profit.
- Don't leave until you have paid back your employer for the knowledge you've gained. It's simply not fair to bolt the moment things are right for you. During much of your employment, you were being paid more than you were worth—because your employer was investing in making you a more valuable employee. Once you become valuable, you need to pay your employer back. What's the arithmetic? No one but you can say. If you want a yardstick, here's one that's as good as any: For every month that you were just ordinary, give your employer a month of extraordinary time. If it took you 18 months to get good, make sure you have worked a total of 36 months before you quit.
- For your own sake, you don't want to tell your boss about your entrepreneurial plans until you know that they work. For his or her sake, you want to find a way to make your new business something your mentor can benefit from. One thing you can do is offer your

employer a stake in the business. It doesn't have to be a controlling interest—the amount depends on how much money you need and how much the employer is willing to put up—but even a small percentage gives him or her a stake in your future growth and prosperity.

- If possible, make the employer's business a client of yours. This is possible if the business you create specializes in some aspect of what your boss is already doing. I've seen many instances of employees successfully going into business this way. With your boss as your first client, you'll be in a great position to get other clients.

- If your employer reacts negatively to your efforts to cut him or her in on your future, don't worry about it. You've done what you can do in terms of giving your boss a chance. Now it's time to take care of your business.

If your goal is to start your own support business, your chances of getting cooperation from your boss should be very high. As financial author Gary North pointed out in his excellent e-zine *Reality Check,* outsourcing yourself can benefit both sides:

Consider an employee who is very good at managing a particular service within a company. No matter how well he does his job, he is unlikely to become the CEO of the company. He is employed to manage a specific component of the overall operation. He maximizes his return for the company by mastering this one operation. He is never going to rise above vice president in charge of this division. If he is ambitious, this fact thwarts his career objectives.

If this in-house service is necessary to companies in the industry, he has a way to advance his career. He can start his own company that specializes in this service. Then he sells this service to several companies in the industry. He maximizes his income. He maximizes his authority. He rises to the top in his own company. He may even rise to the top in his sub-industry. He is no longer facing the career barrier of vice president. ("Outsourcing = Getting Some Help," April 23, 2004, www.garynorth.com)

You can learn more about Gary North and subscribe to *Reality Check,* his free online newsletter, by visiting www.dailyreckoning.com.

HOW TO MAKE YOUR START-UP BUSINESS PROFITABLE IN YEAR ONE

You'll greatly increase your chances for success if you know exactly what you need to do. To make your business profitable in year one, start by figuring out what you need in terms of new-customer revenue, to bring a profit to the bottom line. Then devote at least 80 percent of your resources—your time, your money, and the time and money of your partners and employers—to achieving that new-customer-revenue goal.

The following story illustrates how this is done.

C.F. wanted to open up her own physical therapy business. She had gotten her degree, had spent a year working for other people, and was convinced that the specialty she wanted to practice (pelvic problems in women) had a ready market. She just didn't know how to find it. Nor was she sure of how to set up the administrative part of the business.

We made a deal. I'd act as her "boss" on a consulting basis. We would first agree on long-term, then on one-year, and then on monthly goals. We'd meet every three or four weeks and talk about how to accomplish those goals.

She agreed to work at least 40 hours a week, regardless of

how many patient-hours she had booked. During the first three months, she aimed to book only five appointments. She would spend three hours taking care of administrative expenses and the rest—32 hours—on marketing.

C.F. had not counted on how much time she needed to spend on selling her business, but I convinced her that nothing would happen if she didn't do that. So she did it. She made countless visits to doctors' offices in our community, set up appointments with small social clubs for women, and placed ads.

Neither of us knew anything about marketing professional services at the time, but we didn't let that stop us from going out and pounding the pavement. Initial responses were meager, but, bit by bit, patient by patient, the practice grew.

During the second quarter, from September through November, C.F. increased her paid-for visits to 10 a week. She increased them to 16 during the third quarter and to 21 during the fourth quarter. At 21 visits and 11 hours of administrative work, CF had only eight hours to devote to marketing.

As I said, we met every month—and every month we reviewed the goals and came up with new ideas to attract new patients. We never gave up (though we thought about it more than once). Many of our efforts failed. Yet we persisted. Here and there, we had modest successes that allowed us to meet our relatively conservative objectives and kept C.F. motivated to continue trying.

Finally, we hit on a few marketing concepts that worked—and then an ad that pulled very well. As of our eleventh meeting, the business was making an annualized $120,000 a year and netting half of that.

We agreed on an aggressive back-end plan for the next year and projected revenues in excess of $200,000, with net earnings of about $100,000. That's not bad for a start-up operation

IS WORKING FOR YOURSELF
THE ONLY WAY TO GET RICH?

Contrary to popular mythology, most self-employed business owners are not getting rich. In fact, the average income of small-business owners is virtually the same as that of employees. According to the National Federation of Independent Business (NFIB), both workers and employers make a median income of $30,000.

That's the most common income of both groups, but it doesn't tell the whole story. If you want to know who is making the big bucks—who, for example, is bringing home more than $100,000 a year—the answer is clear: It's the self-employed.

Also, people who employ themselves are more likely than their wage-earning counterparts to move up and down the income scale. When the economy is strong, entrepreneurial earnings go up faster. During recessions, they take a bigger financial hit.

Risk varies for entrepreneurs, depending on where they begin. If you are in the bottom 20 percent of wage earners, starting your own business will probably give you a higher average income than that of the fellow workers you left behind. But if you leave a high-paying job ($60,000 plus), chances are you will end up earning less as a self-employed businessperson than you would sticking with the nine-to-five routine. (Note: This last statistic doesn't belie what I said before about there being more high-income entrepreneurs than employees.)

What does all this mean? Simply this: Quitting your job to go it alone is no guarantee of riches. Most entrepreneurs do no better than employees when it comes to earnings.

The decision to keep a job or go out on your own should be about psychological preferences, not financial ones. You can get rich—or at least achieve financial independence—either way. The

(continues)

trick is to develop a financially valuable skill, to use that skill to achieve a higher-than-average income, to save a good portion of that extra income, and to invest wisely.

So spend a few minutes considering this fundamental question: Will you be happier as an employee or as an entrepreneur? Think about whether it's more important to you to work on your own or with others . . . to have a sense of structure or to enjoy a sense of freedom . . . to have a boss or be one.

There are benefits and drawbacks to both of these work styles. So think about it carefully. It's a very important decision.

in a field—physical therapy—that has a very high new-business mortality rate.

Eleven months after agreeing to follow this program, C.F. was a business success. In a world where more than 90 percent of new ventures fail, hers became profitable in less than a year.

The big point is this: C.F. accomplished what to others must seem like an amazing success—but she did it without performing any miracles.

All she did, really, was follow a long-term program that broke long-term goals down into shorter-term objectives and, finally, into specific tasks. Each individual task was easy: (1) Stop by three doctors' offices and leave brochures, (2) call up certain new mothers' groups and see if they would like her to give a talk, and (3) buy a quarter-page ad in *The Jewish Journal*.

Each task was simple and could be accomplished fairly quickly. If you put them all together—as C.F. did—you can achieve remarkable success in a very short period of time.

We've talked about how to build your knowledge in order to start a new business. We've talked about how to start a business that directly relates to your current field. But you may be wondering what to do when you've finished constructing the foundations and have to actually start earning money.

Well, I have plenty of thoughts on that matter.

NINE IMPORTANT THINGS TO KNOW ABOUT BUSINESS

Apart from starting off with (and sticking to) a good plan, there are nine secrets I've discovered to making a start-up business work.

1. *Business doesn't happen until you make the first sale.* When I first heard this oft-quoted business adage, I found it absurd. There are so many things to do before a sale can be made, I thought, such as setting up an office and installing telephones—not to mention getting the product ready. Later, after I had participated in the stillbirth of dozens of businesses that never had a chance of working in the first place, I realized the wisdom of this axiom. Buying office furniture and printing up business cards don't make a business go. Selling your product does. Yes, there are some preparations you need to take care of before the first sale can be made—but until you have that first check in hand, all you are really doing is spending money.

2. *The most effective way of entering a new market is to offer a popular product at a drastically reduced price.* This was another lesson I bridled against, yet it proved equally important in my business career. In every industry, there is a good market for specialty and high-quality product producers—but capturing a reasonable share of those

137

niche-market segments takes lots of money, time, and experience. When starting a new business, you are likely to be short in those three essentials. That's why it's better to resist the allure of high-priced, prestige products in favor of getting at the big market—selling the most desired products and services at ludicrously cheap prices. It's not always easy to figure out how to undersell the giants. If you can do so, however, you will be in a very happy starting position.

3. *It's ultimately about selling.* Conventional business wisdom says you make money when you buy, not when you sell. I disagree. Although it helps to exercise good judgment in purchasing your product, it doesn't take a genius to do that. Anybody with a modicum of common sense can figure out where the market is and haggle for the right price. Great businesspeople make their fortunes by increasing the perceived value of their products, thus making it possible to ramp up their prices and drastically increase their profit margins. (Think Chanel, Rolex, and Range Rover.)

4. *When choosing a business, select one that can be grown without your personal involvement.* Most professionals, no matter how much they get paid, are wage slaves. And many closely held businesses—especially those built around the personality or drive of a single person—depend for their growth on the commitment of the founder. Avoid getting yourself into this type of business. It flatters the ego but drastically limits your growth potential. In growing your business, make sure it can expand with the addition of more money, property, or people—but not necessarily more of you.

5. *Before you invest time and money in any business, know exactly how much you are willing to lose—and get out if you*

hit that point. We begin new ventures with optimism. That's exactly why we need to plan for the worst. With every business venture you invest in, figure out beforehand how you can get out if things fall apart. And make sure you can afford your exit plan. In stock investing, this is easy enough to do by setting what is called a *stop-loss* point. With other forms of investing—real estate, limited partnerships, and entrepreneurial ventures, for example—it requires more thoughtful planning. Do the planning, and stick with your stop-loss point.

6. *First, improve your strengths. Then, eliminate your weaknesses.* Generally speaking, you will achieve more in business by learning to do better what you already do well than by correcting your weaknesses. If you become a successful real estate broker who is really good at sales presentations but weak on contracts, don't worry so much about getting better at contracts. If necessary, hire someone to handle that part of your business. Spend your self-improvement time advancing from being "really good" to being "really great" at sales presentations. This is not to say you should ignore your weaknesses. We should all strive to eliminate those. But you will find that you'll have more success by attending first to your strengths.

7. *Focused effort is more effective than a diversified approach to business building.* Ambitious people tend to fall into two groups: those who focus almost entirely on one project at a time and those who prefer to spread themselves out on many projects. The focused approach allows you to acquire mastery faster. The diversified approach gives you more balance. In my career, I've taken both approaches. And I have to say that although I'm naturally inclined toward diversification, I've had the most success

and made the most money from the focused work. I believe there is a good reason for that. Success in business comes after you have learned the secrets of the industry you are in. That learning process takes time—four or five thousand hours is the norm. If your attention span is limited and you find yourself jumping too quickly to that other yard (where the grass seems greener), you'll find yourself with too many challenges that you are simply not experienced enough to overcome. If you find that your tendency in business is to skip from one exciting thing to another, train yourself to conquer one field before you set foot in another.

8. *Let your winners run and cut your losses short.* Despite what you may have gleaned about success from listening to entertainers and watching movies, most business ideas or ventures that begin poorly fail. This is a very important lesson to learn. It's very easy to get emotionally attached to projects or investments we believe in. That's why it's so important to follow this rule. When the marketplace tells you that your great idea is a loser, don't keep pushing. Terminate the project and minimize your losses. If it really was a good idea, it will come back to you in the future in another, perhaps better, set of clothing.

9. *Pay attention to Pareto's Law (the 80-20 rule): 80 percent of your success comes from 20 percent of your resources.* This is perhaps the best-known and most useful axiom of success. Most of the success/income/satisfaction you will get in your career will come from a small portion of your skills/projects/efforts. Make it a regular habit to periodically ask yourself "Where am I getting most of the benefit here?" and compare that to where you are putting in the most work.

BUYING AND FLIPPING COMPUTERS

You've heard of buying and flipping real estate—buying a cheap property, fixing it up, and putting it back on the market for a higher price. Jeff Thompson does this with computers.

He started when he was 14, buying cheap computers that he found in the classified section of his local newspaper, putting his skills to work fixing them up, and then selling them in the same paper for a tremendous profit. How tremendous? By the time he was a senior in high school, Jeff's part-time venture—Peripheral Outlet—was generating nearly $8 million a year in revenue. By the time he was a senior in college, the business was making $50 million.

By 1989, the company had switched its focus to computer memory enhancements. Peripheral Outlet's success garnered wide attention, and Thompson was 1994's Young Entrepreneur of the Year. The following year, the company appeared on the Inc. 500 list of America's fastest-growing businesses.

Thompson claims it was his "innate desire" to succeed that propelled him so far in the business world—warning, however, that such single-minded focus can put a strain on personal relationships.

"Talk to as many people as you can," Thompson advises other entrepreneurs. And he stresses the importance of preparing for the obstacles you might encounter before you actually run into them.

Source: Rod M. Lott, "Millionaire Student Learns the 'Why' Behind the 'How' of His Success," Price College of Business Entrepreneurs Feature, Fall 2003.

There may be a few secrets I've forgotten, but these nine would certainly be on my list of the most important things I'd like to teach my children about business.

But what if I could teach them only one secret—the *most* important one?

THAT ONE MOST IMPORTANT THING

I have mentioned my three boys several times already in this book. My oldest son is a computer engineer in the movie industry. My second son is a composer of music. And my third son, still in high school, doesn't yet know what he wants to do.

Is there a single "secret of success" that might be helpful to the three of them, as well as you—given that you all have different interests, hopes, and expectations?

The answer isn't obvious. Like any parent, I want my children to be happy. But there is something else I want—something I've come to understand now that they are getting out in the world and conducting their own affairs: I want them to be good. I want them to have good manners, to treat other people kindly, to be considerate of those who are less fortunate.

When they were youngsters, I wanted them to be good, too, but for pragmatic reasons. I wanted them to behave themselves in the back of the car so I could drive in peace. I wanted them to stay away from the railroad tracks so they wouldn't get killed. And I wanted them to complete their homework assignments so they could learn.

Now I want them to be good for altruistic reasons. I want them to be able to do what my parents wanted me to do: leave the world a little better than they found it. Or better yet, to make their world a little better because they are in it. This is not, I'm sure, an unusual notion. Most parents must feel this way.

So that's what I want—that my children accomplish their goals without sacrificing their fun and become successful without compromising their integrity. I want them to be both good at what they do and good in doing it. Is there something I can tell them that will help them do both?

I think there is. It's a way of conducting yourself in business (and other areas of your life) that can give you success, peace of mind, and happiness. Best of all, perhaps, once learned, it is astonishingly easy to practice.

That secret is this: *In every relationship you get into—every business, social, or personal transaction—make sure the other person gets as much benefit from it as you do. When considering your own advantages and disadvantages in taking any course of action, consider as well those of everyone else involved.*

I realize this idea flies in the face of some thinking. It certainly contradicts the way many prominent corporate executives have been behaving lately. Today the dominant idea of success might be expressed as some version of "looking out for number one."

I've tried that approach, I'm embarrassed to say. In my early years as a marketer, I sold products I wasn't proud of at prices I couldn't justify. I rationalized it all by telling myself I was taking care of my family. That approach didn't work, either in terms of the long-term success of the business or in regard to how I felt about myself.

When I took the initiative to do things right, everything turned out better. Business grew. Relationships developed. And my sense of personal satisfaction skyrocketed.

I realized that by my making my efforts good for everyone else, my eventual success was all but guaranteed. When people begin to see that working with you is something they will benefit from, they are inclined to bring you more and better business deals.

143

Often, focusing on the other person's interests means taking a risk—taking the chance that the time and money you invest in him or her will pay off. To some businesspeople, giving before you get is a foolish idea. For me, it's been the source of all my best and most enjoyed accomplishments.

Let me give you an example of how a colleague of mine, a publisher, put this principle to work. About 10 years ago, he decided he wanted to take over a failing periodical business in England. Instead of doing the "smart" thing—putting the squeeze on the business until it was a breath away from death and then stealing it for pennies on the dollar—he voluntarily moved himself and his family to London for six months to nurse the business back to health. He did this based on nothing more than an oral agreement that if he succeeded in doing that, the London company would then sell him half of the business at some "fair" price.

I was already an advocate of win-win deals at that point in my career, but it seemed to me that this was taking the good-spirited concept to a new level. By fixing the business before he bought it, my colleague was dramatically raising the price he would have to pay for it. He was doing so without compensation. And by doing it all on the basis of an oral contract, he was leaving himself open to being double-crossed.

What happened was very much a happy ending. His new partners got a very nice paycheck for a business they knew was on the verge of bankruptcy. And they returned the favor a few years later when he bought out the rest of their shares by agreeing to the buyout and not haggling over the price.

Today, that business is one of his most productive assets. Just as important, he has great relationships with hundreds of people—employees, vendors, and colleagues—who saw how he behaved and subsequently felt good about doing business with him.

CHAPTER 7

WHY REAL ESTATE IS RIGHT FOR YOU EVEN NOW

WHY YOU SHOULD INVEST IN REAL ESTATE

Next to owning your own business, investing in real estate gives you the highest potential return on investment (ROI). That was true 100 years ago and it is equally true today, even in this world of overinflated property values. The return you get on your investments, as I said in Chapter 2, is one of the three critical keys to developing wealth.

The reason you can get such high returns on real estate is because of the awesome power of financial leverage.

Let me explain. As a real estate investor, you're in the business of buying and selling property. Since property is a relatively easy investment to understand, it's relatively easy to get other people—banks and private investors—to help you out by lending you money. They receive interest payments from you and, initially, loan fees. You get to keep the profits. This is what is called *positive leverage*.

In a typical leveraged (mortgaged) real estate deal, you would invest $20,000 to buy a $100,000 property. If that property appreciates 4 percent (or $4,000), the ROI you achieve is not 4 percent but 20 percent because of the leverage ($4,000 is 20 percent of $20,000).

I'm simplifying things for the moment. But stick with me. This is a pretty interesting subject. If the property provides you with a positive cash flow (i.e., the rent you get for it covers your loan costs plus taxes, insurance, and an allowance for vacancies and maintenance), you benefit from all the appreciation multiplied by the amount of leverage you used.

An 80 percent mortgage (one in which you put up only 20 percent of the property cost) gives you a 5-to-1 leverage advantage. A 90 percent mortgage gives you a 10-to-1 leverage advantage. In a strong real estate market, you may be able to get a 95 percent loan, which equates to an 18-to-1 leverage advantage. When you can combine the advantages of buying "right" and borrowing with a reasonable price appreciation, you can make a lot of money. For example, let's say you got a good buy on a $100,000 property (i.e., it had a market value of $120,000). And let's say, too, that you put $10,000 down and waited five years to sell it. If the average appreciation (rise in property values) during that five-year period was 5 percent (a historical average), then your gross profit (sale price less purchasing price) would be $46,000. If you subtract buying and selling costs of about $12,000, you have a net profit of $34,000. Turning $10,000 into $34,000 in five years is a pretty impressive financial feat. It would be hard to replicate that with stocks (without being enormously lucky and taking great risk). It would be impossible to do as well with bonds. Real estate investing—if you do it right—gives you the chance to make 25-plus percent ROI with very modest risk (even in today's overhyped markets).

LITTLE WORK, BIG RETURNS

Another big advantage that real estate offers you is time. You can invest in real estate on a very, very part-time basis.

I'm a good example. My business time is devoted to my business, which is helping people sell things. I've made millions from my business interests, but I've made as much or more from real estate. I've earned good income from real estate by buying and selling homes and condos—even raw land. And I've also "gotten richer while I sleep" by buying rental properties and holding on to them until their rents exceeded their expenses.

When I look at my personal financial history, I can see that real estate has been my biggest wealth-building investment. Yet in the 15 or so years I've been actively investing in it, I've spent an average of only about two hours a week working on it!

You can see why I like real estate.

But I'm not the only one. Many of my friends, colleagues, and protégés have gotten rich through real estate. For example:

- D.L. started out by buying and flipping a single-family home. He now specializes in apartment buildings and currently has over 600 cash-producing units. Part of the transition for D.L. was cashing out of his red-hot Massachusetts market and moving into other areas of the country that have far better rental yields and greater appreciation potential. He continues to make money despite bubble markets in much of the country.
- J.F. has made very good money in the South Florida real

estate market (including one property on which he and I are partners). But he's also expanding into other markets. Specifically, he's targeting areas with strong employment and population growth that still have good rental yields. And he's looking into areas where the price of the median home is only 2.5 to 3 times the median income (as opposed to such prices being nearly 6 times the median income in California).

- G.L. got into this business two years ago, and he's making a decent living with his "bad neighborhood" investments. He turns over an average of three or four properties a year at a $20,000 profit for each. And not long ago, he fixed up a $170,000 house that he moved into himself. When he was offered $275,000 for it a year later, he happily vacated.

- B.M. (a guy who has mastered the "art" of buying and selling expensive cars, watches, etc.) bought two preconstruction condominium units in our town for $265,000 each. The property is not yet finished, but all the units have already been sold. The last six were sold for more than $300,000 each. B.M. has made almost $100,000 in less than 18 months.

And then, of course, there are the legendary real estate barons. Forbes.com lists the following real estate investors as some of the richest men in the world.

- *Donald Bren:* With a $10,000 loan, he was able to build his first house. In 1977, he purchased the Irvine Company—a real estate development company—with 34 other investors. By 1996, Bren was the sole owner of the company. He owns the Irvine Ranch, selling one-acre lots for more than $1 million each. Bren is also the owner of some 400 office buildings, 35 shopping centers, 80 apartment complexes, and 2 luxury hotels. *Net worth: $4.3 billion.*

- *Donald Trump:* While he is most recently known for his hit reality series *The Apprentice,* real estate accounts for the majority of Trump's wealth. He owns over 18 million square feet of prime Manhattan space, including 40 Wall Street, Trump World Tower, and Trump International Hotel & Tower. He is also in charge of the successful West Side rail yard residential development. Purchased for $80 million in 1985, it now sells for over $2,000 per square foot. *Net worth: $2.6 billion.*

- *Samuel Zell:* In the 1960s, Zell began buying and flipping cheap apartment buildings. He got a deal on rehabilitation prices due to the rising cost of new-building construction. The Chicago-based real estate mogul now owns 125 million square feet of office space and 202,000 apartments. *Net worth: $2.2 billion.*

- *William Pulte:* At the age of 18, in 1950, Pulte built his first home. Two years later, he founded Pulte Homes, which is now the nation's largest home builder, with more than 408,000 homes under its belt. His company continues to expand throughout the United States and into Mexico and Puerto Rico. *Net worth: $1.5 billion.*

- *John Sobrato:* In 1957, he began selling homes as a college student. His successes encouraged him to branch into commercial real estate. Sobrato's business controls more than 10 million square feet, making him one of Silicon Valley's largest commercial landlords. *Net worth: $1.5 billion.*

- *Thomas Flatley:* Flatley opened his own development company in 1959 and has since built over 1,400 apartment buildings. He sold his apartment portfolio in 2002 for

149

$500 million but continues to control 8 million square feet of commercial and retail space, including office buildings, nursing homes, drive-in restaurants, industrial buildings, and many acres of commercial land. *Net worth: $1.2 billion.*
*   *Walter H. Shorenstein:* He joined the brokerage firm Milton Meyer & Company in 1946. Becoming a partner in 1951, Shorenstein went on to become president and sole owner of the renamed Shorenstein Company in 1960. The company partly managed and owned over 20 million square feet of real estate across the United States until 2004, when it sold some of its San Francisco properties. *Net worth: $750 million.*

WHAT CAN YOU EXPECT FROM REAL ESTATE?

As a recent graduate (or young person), real estate offers you a tremendous opportunity. That's because you don't need a lot of money to get started and you can use your youth (the many years you have to let your investments appreciate) to work in your favor.

Let's run through the numbers quickly.

Real estate, historically, provides a 6 percent average ROI. That number is composed of 4 percent in equity appreciation (how much the price of the building increases over time) and 2 percent in net rental income (what you get from rents after all expenses). Both figures are probably low. Several studies put equity appreciation at 5 percent or 6 percent, while net rental income, if you manage your properties the right way, could easily be 4 percent or 5 percent. If you based your expectations on recent history, you would expect much higher numbers. Between 1995 and 2005, property appreciation in many parts of the country was 15 percent or 20 percent per year.

That's not likely to happen in the next 10 years. Prices have slowed and will continue to do so. But if you invest carefully in areas where that population boom will take place (the U.S. Census Bureau predicts that California, Florida, and Texas will experience significant population growth in the next 20 years), you should see ROIs in the 5 percent to 6 percent range. By studying the particular market you're buying in, you'll be able to buy property "right" (at below-market prices)—that will ratchet up your ROIs even further.

For the purposes of this discussion, we are going to talk about a real estate investment strategy that will allow you to get rich on an average ROI of only 6 percent.

In case you are wondering how real estate, with a 6 percent return, can make you rich, remember the power of leverage. When you ratchet up that 6 percent by using a 20 percent mortgage, the return you get from your investment is more likely to be in the 25 percent to 30 percent range.

In Chapter 2, I recommended that you devote 15 percent of your income, starting this year, to your goal of becoming wealthy. A portion of that 15 percent (I'd recommend either a third or a half) should be put in real estate. Let's take another look at the tables we saw in Chapter 2 but this time focus on only real estate. Even if we use the lowest figures for your income—if you were to make an average base salary for a college grad with a 4 percent annual increase in income—your investments would have astronomical returns.

Table 7.1 shows you how much you'd make if you invested 5 percent of your income in real estate. Over $3 million after 25 years of investing, and over $8.6 billion if you continue to invest for 55 years. Pretty impressive, huh?

Table 7.2 shows you what would happen if you invested half the 15 percent (or 7.5 percent) into real estate. Again, the numbers are impressive: Twenty-five years of investing has

TABLE 7.1

**Example of Wealth Built Up by a Real Estate Investor
(with 5% of His or Her Income Invested with a 30% ROI)**

Year	Age	Income (with 4% Annual Increase)	Deposit (5% of Income)	30% Interest on Deposit + Previous Year's Total	Total Value of Investment
1	22	$30,337.00	$1,516.85	$455.06	$1,213.48
5	26	$35,490.00	$1,774.50	$2,893.37	$11,650.70
10	31	$43,179.01	$2,158.95	$13,502.90	$57,433.10
15	36	$52,533.87	$2,626.69	$53,493.30	$230,490.96
20	41	$63,915.48	$3,195.77	$202,702.37	$876,779.04
25	46	$77,762.96	$3,888.15	$757,590.32	$3,280,947.32
30	51	$94,610.53	$4,730.53	$2,818,927.35	$12,212,986.60
35	56	$115,108.17	$5,755.41	$10,473,837.67	$45,383,752.19
40	61	$140,046.69	$7,002.33	$38,897,577.90	$168,552,669.71
45	66	$170,388.22	$8,519.41	$144,434,875.13	$625,880,199.21
50	71	$207,303.32	$10,365.17	$536,289,831.79	$2,323,917,421.86
55	76	$252,216.19	$12,610.81	$1,991,222,726.86	$8,628,625,510.98

turned your initial deposit into nearly $5 million. And after 55 years, you end up with close to $13 billion. These figures should persuade you that investing in real estate is something you should seriously consider.

And keep in mind that these tables don't account for a radical increase in your income. If you're making $150,000 by the time you're 25 and go on to make $1 million by age 32, the total value of your investment would leap through the ceiling. Investing 5 percent of your income, with 30 percent returns, you'd have close to $4 million in 20 years and $41 billion in 55 years. And if you invested 7.5 percent of your radically

TABLE 7.2

**Example of Wealth Built Up by a Real Estate Investor
(with 7.5% of His or Her Income Invested with a 30% ROI)**

Year	Age	Income (with 4% Annual Increase)	Deposit (7.5% of Income)	30% Interest on Deposit + Previous Year's Total	Total Value of Investment
1	22	$30,337.00	$2,275.28	$682.58	$1,820.22
5	26	$35,490.00	$2,661.75	$4,340.06	$17,476.05
10	31	$43,179.01	$3,238.43	$20,254.35	$86,149.65
15	36	$52,533.87	$3,940.04	$80,239.95	$345,736.43
20	41	$63,915.48	$4,793.66	$304,053.55	$1,315,168.56
25	46	$77,762.96	$5,832.22	$1,136,385.48	$4,921,420.98
30	51	$94,610.53	$7,095.79	$4,228,391.03	$18,319,479.90
35	56	$115,108.17	$8,633.11	$15,710,756.50	$68,075,628.28
40	61	$140,046.69	$10,503.50	$58,346,366.84	$252,829,004.57
45	66	$170,388.22	$12,779.12	$216,652,312.70	$938,820,298.82
50	71	$207,303.32	$15,547.75	$804,434,747.69	$3,485,876,132.78
55	76	$252,216.19	$18,916.21	$2,986,834,090.29	$12,942,938,266.47

increased income, you'd have nearly $6 million after 20 years and a staggering $62 billion in 55 years.

Are you convinced yet that real estate is the way to go?

ISN'T IT HARD TO GET STARTED?

I've been trying to persuade my older sons, both of whom are recent graduates, to invest in real estate. By now (after all my orating), they understand the numbers. They know—in their heads, they know—that real estate is something they should invest in. But they haven't yet started to do it. Why?

I think there are several reasons:

- Lack of knowledge about the details
- Fear of the unknown
- Reluctance to try something new
- A wee bit of laziness

All that is understandable. Those are the same reasons I delayed getting into real estate for 20 years.

But if you could overcome those reservations, what a great advantage you would have! Here's the thing you need to know: *Investing in real estate is really very easy.* Yes, there are little things you'll need to learn. But don't worry about them now. You'll pick them up as you go along. And, yes, you'll be doing something that's new to you. But don't worry about that, either. You'll like it! Once you buy your first property, the next purchase will be much, much easier.

Everyone I know who has gotten into real estate started with just one property and a great deal of hesitation and—just a year or two later—had at least a half dozen properties and was very comfortable about buying more.

In the following pages, we are going to take a look at the fundamentals of real estate: what sort of investments there are, how you can get into them, what "rules" you should follow, and so on.

FOUR APPROACHES TO REAL ESTATE INVESTING

The four easiest ways to make substantial returns in real estate are the following:

1. Buying and selling fixer-uppers
2. Buying and flipping new properties
3. Investing in a local limited partnership
4. Buying and managing local rental properties

Let's look at each of these in detail.

Buying and Selling Fixer-Uppers

Buying and selling fixer-uppers may be the best-known way of making money in real estate. The no-money-down real estate gurus tend to focus on this area because the numbers can look very good, especially when you get into low-income housing.

BUYING PROPERTIES IN "BAD" NEIGHBORHOODS

It's not as fast and easy as some say, but it can work. If you're on a tight budget and want to start with inexpensive properties, you'll be buying houses in the poorest part of town. That will make you (from some perspectives) the worst kind of capitalist pig—one that "gentrifies" ethnic neighborhoods.

Poor neighborhoods are generally ethnic neighborhoods, so unless you are of the group you are "exploiting," you'll probably be categorized as some sort of local robber baron. You'll know how ridiculous such thinking is. But your neighbor—the woman who went to Vassar and makes a living promoting rich-lady wine-tasting tours in Tuscany—will secretly despise you. Oh, well.

Meanwhile, you will be kept busy doing the following:

- Studying the neighborhood before you buy into it.
- Buying a cheap house, even by local standards.
- Fixing it up to sell it fast.
- Selling it to the first person who buys, regardless of race,

creed, or color (that's the part that will make people think you're un-American).

In order to make this a part-time business, you'll have to develop a network of workers—reliable tradespeople who won't overcharge you—to take care of all the fixing up. They should be the same folks you'll use for the rental properties we'll talk about later. So if you eventually decide to go into both businesses—investing in rental real estate and buying and selling fixer-uppers—you'll be able to keep them pretty busy.

From what I've learned—from my own investing, from my reading, and most of all from Justin Ford, *Early to Rise*'s (*www.earlytorise.com*) resident expert on real estate—there are two things you should do to make this type of investing profitable:

1. *Don't hunt and peck for houses.* Target a specific area and plan to eventually buy up many, if not most, of the homes in it. That way, you will get the benefit of having a neighborhood go up in value along with the individual units you are buying.
2. *If you can, select a target area that has at least one border on the outside.* By "border," I mean a better neighborhood. Giving your potential buyers the feeling that they are buying into a section of a neighborhood with a corridor to safety will increase—significantly—the value of every house in that section. It will also give you a wider market. (This is where you'll be accused of gentrification.)

What you look for in terms of structure in a buy-and-sell situation is very different from what you look for when you are buying rental property. When you are going to be a landlord, you should buy a property that has no significant structural problems (roofing, plumbing, and so on). For a buy-and-sell home, you simply should make sure everything is working now and will be working for another year or so. The more important consideration—at least from the profit angle—is how much under the market price you can buy it for.

What you should do is buy a $60,000 home in a neighborhood where most of the homes sell for $75,000, make it look 100 percent better for about $5,000, and then sell it for $73,000 in less than three months. Sometimes, you'll be able to do better than that. But don't hold on to a property for more than 90 days if you can possibly avoid it. Even if you make a smaller profit—say, $5,000 to $10,000—it's better to get out of a slow-selling house and into another that will sell quickly.

In the buy-and-sell real estate business, it's all about moving quickly.

That also pertains to the fixing-up you'll be doing. Don't take on anything that might require long-term renovation. Avoid bad roofs, serious electrical problems, and "issues" with sewage or flooding.

Spend your money on quick-and-easy stuff like painting, landscaping, and carpeting. If you can't make the property look considerably more valuable with such cosmetic changes, you probably shouldn't buy it.

Keep in mind that you don't *have to* start at the bottom. If you have more money to invest, you can do all of the above in a better neighborhood. In fact, if you can, I'd advise it.

BUYING PROPERTIES IN BETTER NEIGHBORHOODS

The higher the level of the fixer-upper you can buy, the more money you're going to make. So start where you need to and graduate to more expensive properties as you go. Neighborhoods tend to be priced within certain ranges. But

157

those ranges are determined by percentages, not absolute numbers.

Generally speaking, the range is about 30 percent. That means that in a neighborhood of homes with a mean selling price of $90,000, the vast majority of individual homes would be priced between, say, $75,000 and $105,000. A neighborhood of homes with a mean selling price of $60,000 would have a range between $50,000 and $70,000. And one with a mean selling price of $400,000 would have a range between $340,000 and $460,000.

BUYING PROPERTIES IN REALLY GOOD NEIGHBORHOODS

I know a lot of builders. And many of them play the musical-home game. It goes like this: They buy a relatively inexpensive home in a pricey neighborhood (say, a $550,000 home in a $700,000 neighborhood). They move in and fix it up over a period of time—usually six months to a year. They can't really afford to live in such an expensive home, but everything is a write-off. Besides, they have plans.

Soon after everything is finished, along comes a buyer—and they are "forced" to sell the home for a $150,000 profit. They invest that money in their next home—a $750,000 home in a $950,000 neighborhood.

One of these guys just moved into my neighborhood. He has put—as near as I can tell—about $1.7 million into a house that could easily fetch $2.7 million. He hasn't told his neighbors that it's up for sale, but I know two brokers who are showing it privately. This is a guy who was living in a $65,000 town house 10 years ago.

Buying and Flipping Preconstruction Properties

Given the state of the real estate market today, I do not recommend buying preconstruction condominiums. The condo

SUCCESS AND HAPPINESS AT THE SAME TIME

In 1999, Jonathan Safran Foer left college with a bachelor's degree in philosophy. Three short years later, the hardcover rights for his senior thesis—a novel—made him $500,000 richer. Midway through 2002, HarperCollins fattened Foer's bank account once again when they purchased the paperback rights for *Everything Is Illuminated* for $925,000. Only 25, and already a millionaire.

In a 2003 interview with Robert Birnbaum of identity theory.com, Foer noted that Joyce Carol Oates, his mentor and former professor, helped him understand his talents—and propelled his career as a writer forward. "She was the first person ever to make me think I should try to write in any sort of serious way," Foer told Birnbaum. She also opened his eyes to what she deemed "the most important of writerly qualities, energy."

Foer told Birnbaum that he endured many rejections before Houghton Mifflin picked him up—so he strongly believes that persistence is crucial for success. To succeed at anything worthwhile, you have to keep pushing and pushing until someone recognizes your potential.

While in college, Foer had no inkling as to which career path he should pursue. Instead, he found that he was constantly discovering what he did not want to do. But he didn't worry about his lack of focus. "I felt very strongly that there was something inside of me, something that I wanted to express," Foer told Birnbaum. He didn't know exactly what that "something" was—but with the help of his mentor, he discovered that his future success lay in doing something he had always loved to do: write.

Sources: Clark Collis, "Foer Play," *The Observer*, June 2, 2002; "Jonathan Safran Foer," May 26, 2003.

market has been the market that has taken the biggest hit when real estate has been devalued. And there's good reason for that. Condos are generally cheaper than single-family homes, and therefore they attract the less experienced investors who flood into the market after prices have already gone sky-high. Adding fuel to the fire, condominiums are often overbuilt—many more units are built than the local market can afford.

Both those phenomena are occurring now, as I'm writing this. All the top real estate guys I know, including the bankers, are getting very nervous about condos. By the time you read this, prices may already be falling. If so, accumulate your cash for when the market bottoms out, so you can get in at the bottom.

If the market hasn't deflated yet, I'd recommend that you buy cautiously. Look for single-family homes and prime commercial properties. Stay away from condos. And stay far, far away from the temptation to buy and sell preconstruction condos.

The reason people like to buy preconstruction condos and sell them is that you can market them as "new" property (always more in demand) and never have to worry about maintenance or condo fees. This is a nice way to make money. No mess, no hassle. But in an overvalued market that topples, condominiums fall the furthest and the fastest. When the market gets better (as it surely will), then you can use the following advice to help you make money with preconstruction investing.

First, stick with developments in your hometown because you'll have a pretty good idea about which direction prices are going. You may not yet know how to determine beforehand whether *individual* developments are good, but keep these criteria in mind:

- The developer has to have an established track record and good references.
- The location has to be one that is very good or moving up.
- There shouldn't be anything seriously wrong with the development (such as a lack of adequate parking or a proximity to railroad tracks).
- The size of the development should be appropriate to the local market (with neither too many units nor too few).

A Few Words of Caution

Buying and selling real estate won't work if property values are falling. So if prices are heading down when you read this, wait for a while till they seem to have steadied. My guess is that single-family homes will drop about 15 percent, town houses 20 percent to 25 percent, and condos 25 percent to 50 percent. Keep that in mind when you try to figure out if the market has hit bottom.

One great thing about real estate: It goes up much more often than it goes down. And the good properties in the good areas go up much stronger and longer than the rest.

Buying and selling real estate is a great way to make good money, but it's *not* something you can do all the time.

You should determine for yourself whether properties are appreciating in your area. If they are, look around and see whether there are units you can buy that meet your own financial requirements. The better you can judge the market, the less risk you take and the better advantage you can take of the power of leverage.

Here are a few more tips on buying and selling real estate:

- If you have to rehab the property, remember that this is not the time to create your dream house. Focus only on the areas that would bring up a red flag at closing and the relatively inexpensive things that will help the house show better—such as fresh paint, new windows, landscaping, and a thorough cleaning.

- Don't get emotionally caught up in a fast-rising market. The most common mistake people have made when they lose money flipping a property is that they paid too much for it, expecting that the price would skyrocket. If prices stall and you don't have a rental yield to cover your costs, you could be looking at a loss.
- Don't be looking to flip properties if you are always in a crunch for money. You could become a "desperate" investor—and you never want to buy or sell in desperation.

As a novice, you should severely limit your investment. That said, wouldn't it be nice to have a little part-time, buy-and-flip business that could give you $20,000, $50,000 or even $100,000 a year in extra cash flow?

Investing in a Local Limited Partnership

If you talked to a financial planner about real estate investing, he or she might suggest that you invest either in REITs (real estate investment trusts) or limited partnerships.

I don't like either one for college graduates who are new to the financial markets. Here's why:

- REITs are like stocks. You have no control over them, you have little chance to interact with management, and your knowledge of the business and its prospects is likely to be based on the information the business gives you. When you invest in an REIT, you are gambling on very limited information. That might be appropriate for a very small part of your stock portfolio (for balance), but it's not the kind of investing that gives me comfort.

- Legally, a limited partnership is a passive investment. As a part-time partner, you generally go in as a limited partner. That means (1) the money you risk is limited to the money you put in (you can't incur any further obligations) and (2) the money you get out will probably be less, proportionately, than the money the general partners take out.

There are many ways you can get cheated when you give your money to a real estate developer. For example:

- General partners can use the electrician your deal is paying for to do some work on their own homes or on another project. You pay the bill for both jobs but get the benefit of only one. Since this is done entirely with a wink and a nod, you won't have any way of knowing that it's happening. And even if you did, you would have no way to prove it.
- You can put your money into a deal that never gets off the ground. General partners can take your initial investment, make the money disappear into some inflated subcontractor bills, declare bankruptcy, and walk away, leaving the job unfinished.
- You can get screwed by the lawyers, bankers, and brokers as well.

It's a messy, complicated business—and everybody has an angle. Still, it can be a very good part-time business for you if you are dealing with honest partners in a good market. In one case recently, for example, I doubled my money in 18 months by investing in some high-end homes in Snowmass, Colorado. In another deal—one in Florida that I got into four years ago—I ended up making (though not the 25 percent projected) 15 percent over a four-year period on a considerable stake. In the latter case, the general partner apologized for the performance. I was quite happy with it.

The most important rule about investing in limited partnerships is to know and trust your partners. If you aren't 100 percent certain you'll be treated fairly, either don't get involved at all or invest only what you can easily afford to lose.

The next-most-important rule is to get actively involved on a part-time basis. By this, I mean you should carefully review the contract, compare it with others, speak to outside experts, get to know the other limited partners, arrange regular interviews with the general partners, study the building plans, go to the job sites, and so on. Make it clear from the start that you intend to be a very active passive partner. If they are good people, they will agree to it. But they will probably want to set some reasonable limits so they don't end up spending all their time with you.

In addition to doing all that, you'll need to make sure that the contract is written fairly. "Fairly" means that (1) the limited partners get their money out of the deal before the general partners do, (2) the general partners are not double-dipping by charging large management fees, (3) the projected ROIs are reasonable and appended to the contract, (4) you have the right to sue them if you feel you must, and (5) all the partners (general and limited) put actual green cash in the bank—and leave it there throughout the life of the deal.

But the ultimate consideration is trust. Never, ever invest in a limited partnership (of any sort) that's run by someone with whom you don't have an established working relationship unless you can afford to (emotionally and financially) suffer a loss.

There's that old saying: When two people get together for business and one has the money and the other has the knowledge, at the end of the deal the guy with the money has the knowledge and the guy with the knowledge has the money.

Buying and Managing Local Rental Properties

My first experience in real estate was an unforgettable disaster. My wife and I were living in a little town house in the Dupont Circle area of Washington, D.C. I had just come back from a two-year Peace Corps stint in Africa and was working as a journalist for a small international newsletter-publishing business on K Street.

With the expenses (some welcomed, some not) of an unplanned newborn, a long-ago-planned graduate school education, and an underestimated (after two years of living in a mud hut) modern American lifestyle, my wife and I were financially strained. Still, my landlady convinced me that I should be a property owner. She sold me a condominium apartment in a building she had just developed. It didn't cost me much up front, but the monthly bills were pretty stiff.

The condo turned out to be too small to live in, so we decided to rent it out. And that's when my real-life education in real estate started.

Counting taxes, upkeep, and my mortgage, I realized that the condo was costing me about $950 a month. When I put it on the rental market, I soon discovered it would fetch only $550. That left me cash-negative by $400 a month, or $5,000 a year. Since I couldn't afford that, I put the condo up for sale—but discovered that the amount I still owed the bank (it might have been $68,000) exceeded the property's actual market value by about $15,000.

Talk about being on the horns of a dilemma! My choice was to keep the condo and "lose" $400 a month, which I could barely afford to do, or sell it and lose $15,000 on the spot, which I couldn't do.

So I couldn't sell it. I had to cut back on our other expenses and hope the market would get better.

Three years later, when I was $15,000 out of pocket, the market hadn't changed. And my real estate deal was about to get worse.

The loan was a three-year balloon. That meant that every three years, I had to either pay it back in full (which I could not afford to do) or refinance it—which meant higher fees and closing costs. That first closing, if I remember correctly, my monthly out-of-pocket expense increased to $450. And for the privilege of paying that extra $50, I had to come up with $1,500 in closing costs!

Of course, I considered refinancing with another bank. But I soon discovered that my loan was backed by neither Freddie Mac nor Fannie Mae. Without government backing, no other bank would go near it. I was stuck with the crooks I had signed my first contract with. They wouldn't give me anything but three-year balloons, because that's how they could get the most money out of me. They were making a lot of money on property that wasn't worth much, and every three years they got to jack up the payments and charge me for their time to do it.

If I told you that was the end of it, you'd surely pity me. But it was actually worse. My loan, you see, was negatively amortized. That meant that at the end of the three years, the amount I owed—if I wanted to buy out the mortgage in cash—was higher than it had been three years earlier. After I paid the bank more than $5,000 in mortgage payments and another $15,000 in closing costs, my $68,000 mortgage was now $72,000!

I was in real estate hell. And it wasn't until I decided to make money—and actually made some—that I could afford to pay off the crooks and get myself out of it. The whole lesson, in total, cost me $35,000 and six years of living at least $400 a month poorer than I should have.

Oh . . . one more thing. The sweet girl I rented to turned out to be a hooker who was bringing her trade up to the apartment day and night, which made the neighbors complain constantly. I couldn't kick her out, I was advised, because the laws in D.C. were set up to protect innocent tenants from evil landlords.

HOW TO MAKE RENTAL REAL ESTATE WORK FOR YOU

It seems to me that there are two big secrets in making rental real estate work for you. One has to do with the old "location/location/location" axiom. The other is about the condition of the property you buy.

Let's start with some rules, keeping in mind that rules are made to be followed until you understand the principles behind them.

Buy Properties in Your Local Area

To be a successful investor, you have to know what you are doing. And if you have been living where you are living for any number of years, you already have more knowledge about local real estate than you think. You already have a clear idea of the good neighborhoods, the not-so-good ones, and the ones you need to stay out of. You may have developed a feeling for the up-and-comers. By staying in your local area, you give yourself the chance to really know the market. And that is the most important factor in limiting your risk and increasing your chances for profits.

Invest in Good or Up-and-Coming Properties

I can tell you from experience that the old saying about the three rules of real estate being "location, location, location" is true. But there are two kinds of good locations: those that are already established as good and those that are on their way to becoming good. You can make money with both.

Here's how . . .

- In good neighborhoods, buy the least-expensive property you can find. That way, any money you spend fixing it up (if you fix it up wisely) will bring you double or triple your invested dollars. When you buy a poor piece of property in a good neighborhood, you get the benefit of the neighborhood to lift your selling price once the property looks acceptable. Of course, it's not easy to get the least-expensive piece of property in such a good neighborhood cheap. Most of the time, the property owner realizes what's going on. But with really dilapidated homes, and sometimes with owner-sold properties, you can get a real bargain.

  A quick example: A couple of years ago, I bought a 1,200-square-foot, two-bedroom apartment in my hometown for $62,000 and rented it out for $1,000 a month. That's a very good deal, even after considering the three grand I spent fixing it up.

- In up-and-coming neighborhoods, buy properties in clusters—either by yourself or with a consortium of buyers. That way, when they are all renovated, the look of the entire area will be upgraded. This will bring up prices, sometimes more than you'd guess.

- Whenever possible, buy newer, solid structures. There's nothing worse than managing a run-down building. The tenants complain. They are reluctant to pay the rent. They treat you like a crook. It's bad. Be extra careful about the critical and costly things. Don't buy any property that has major problems—a bad roof, rotten plumbing, or burned-out electrical wiring. The cost will eat up any profit you can make.
- Develop a network of reliable contractors: a plumber, an electrician, an air-conditioning person, a painter, a landscaper, and—most important—an inexpensive handyman. They should be the same folks we talked about earlier—the ones who'll help renovate your fixer-uppers as well as the properties you flip.

As in so many businesses, real estate is all about buying the right way. If you get a property for a good price and don't overinvest in fixing it up, you'll be 95 percent certain to do well in the long run.

My own very general guideline on buying rental properties is never to buy a property if the total cost (sales price plus fix-up expenses) exceeds nine times the rent. Usually, I try to do—and do—better than that, though that's not easy in good and up-and-coming markets where there is a lot of sophisticated competition vying for limited properties.

Say, for example, you found a building that could be bought for $90,000. And say it would require $10,000 to bring it up to what you want it to be. (What you want it to be is in a condition that will enable you to get a decent rent and keep your tenants from complaining because things are breaking all the time.) That's $100,000 total. In such a situation, following my rules, you'd want your total monthly rents to be $11,000 or more.

Say you could get $11,500. Here's how it would look, from an investment perspective, if you paid for everything in cash: Your total investment would be $100,000, and your net cash flow, after paying property taxes (say, $1,000 a year) and upkeep (say, $1,500 a year), would be $9,000. That's a 9 percent return on your money. That's a pretty good deal if you believe, as I do, that real estate is safer than stocks.

That's not the whole story, however. If you buy the right way and in the right location, you'll get a very significant appreciation in the property value. This can vary widely. Historically, it's been about 4 percent to 5 percent—which would give you a total cash return of about 13 percent to 14 percent.

But that's just the average. If you know what you are doing, you can do much better than that. A rental property I bought three years ago for $195,000 just sold for $395,000. My ROI was astronomical.

I think you understand the point. Owning rental properties—if you own good ones (which translates into better tenants and fewer complaints)—can be a very manageable way to make a lot of extra money on the side, while you are working for someone else or running your own business.

YOU MAKE YOUR MONEY BY BUYING THE RIGHT WAY

One of the most successful real estate investors I know is Frank McKinney, who lives in my area. He started by learning as much as he could about real estate by reading everything on the subject that he could get his hands on. He researched the local market and attended foreclosure auctions for 10 months. Then he scraped together some money and bought his first property. It was a roach-infested former crack house in a run-down part

FOUR WEALTH-BUILDING FACTORS IN REAL ESTATE

Four factors in real estate transactions combine to build wealth for you as a real estate investor: *appreciation, leverage, net rents,* and *amortization.* And the first one, appreciation, isn't simple appreciation—it's *compounded appreciation.*

Let's say you buy a property for $100,000 that is appreciating at an annual rate of 6.5 percent. In the first year, it goes up $6,500. But in year 11, your *annual* 6.5 percent appreciation works out to $12,200. Why? Because the value of the property has compounded to about $187,700. The 6.5 percent increase in the value of the property in year 11 is $12,200, not just $6,500.

You *leverage* that with financing. You originally put 10 percent down ($10,000) plus another $2,000 in closing costs. *The appreciation in year 11 alone would work out to be more than 100 percent of your original investment* (since $12,200 is more than 100 percent of your original $12,000 total initial investment).

Net rents are the profits you make on property you rent after subtracting all your costs on the loan and maintenance. While net rents may seem small when you first invest in a rental property, they quickly become a significant source of income.

Amortization is simply the equity you gain each month as the balance on the property loan declines. So if you originally borrowed $90,000, at the end of year 1 that balance may be just $88,000 (depending on your interest rate and amortization schedule). And by year 10, you may have picked up an extra $12,000 to $15,000 this way—even before taking appreciation or leverage into account.

There are a dozen or so ways of making a fortune in real estate. And all four of these wealth-building factors are present in most of them.

of town. He picked it up for $30,000, fixed it up, and sold it just a few months after buying it—for a profit of nearly $20,000.

Frank went on to consummate hundreds of these types of deals, eventually flipping dozens of properties in a single year.

So, what are some proven strategies for doing that—buying and selling property quickly?

First, make sure you buy at a good price. If you can snatch up a property for significantly below its current market value, chances are you'll be able to easily turn it around and sell it for a nice profit.

It's difficult to become an expert on the value of real estate all over town, so focus on one or two neighborhoods that you are familiar with. Properties that are selling at a discount to market value won't last long, so you'll have to do some legwork to uncover deals and be ready to jump on bargains the moment they appear.

Look through your local paper and call a dozen homes for sale in and around your neighborhood. Initially, just stick to single-family homes and simply find out the address, asking price, and square footage of each. Don't bother with kitchen upgrades and the pretty garden—those are details that don't matter unless you get the price per square foot right first.

Also, when you ask for square footage keep in mind that there are *two types:* "total" and "under air" square footage. "Total," not surprisingly, refers to all structures, while "under air" refers only to those parts of the house that are heated or cooled. (It doesn't, for example, include the garage, porch, storage shed, and similar structures.) Either number will do as long as—when you're comparing properties—you compare "under air" to "under air" and "total" to "total." You need to compare apples to apples, in other words.

Then you're going to check another dozen homes. Not homes for sale this time, but homes that have recently sold—preferably within the last 12 months. Some local papers list this information. If yours doesn't, simply contact your county property appraiser's office. This is public information and very easy to get. In fact, most county records are online and you can do some very useful research very quickly with a few clicks of a mouse.

Once you've completed these two tasks, begin to figure out prices per square foot in your neighborhood. For instance, if sellers are asking $150,000 for a home in your neighborhood that has only 1,200 square feet, they're asking $125 per square foot ($150,000/1,200 = $125). But when you go into the homes that have already sold, you may find the average per-square-foot price has been only $100 over the last 12 months. This can not only help you weed the bargains from the bubbles but also help you determine whether an overall neighborhood might be on the verge of peaking or just about to take off.

Finally, get rent quotes for a dozen properties in the same area. Try to get quotes for two- and three-bedroom homes for rent, though (if need be) half your quotes can be for two- and three-bedroom apartments. In all cases, write down square footage along with the monthly rent.

Use a spreadsheet to map out the details of each sold or rented property, including the square footage. By dividing the sale price by the square footage, you get the cost per square foot. By averaging all of your results, you will get the average cost per square foot for homes that have recently sold in your area.

Next, put together a list of the homes that are for sale or for rent right now. Do the same sort of calculation (using asking price instead of sale price) to come up with the average current asking price per square foot of property in your area.

Armed with these numbers, you now have a reliable benchmark to help you quickly determine whether a property represents a good value and a potentially profitable investment.

Once you know the property values in your target area stone-cold, you are ready to recognize true bargains the moment they appear.

Scour the paper every day or two and call about every property for sale. You can also do some valuable research on www.realtor.com. When you have the address, square footage, and asking price, compare it with the comparable values you've already established for the area.

FOUR TRICKS FOR FINDING
AVAILABLE REAL ESTATE

Look for telltale signs that owners may be thinking of selling, even before they advertise the property.

1. *The home-alone technique.* Whenever you see a vacant home in your target area, stop to jot down the address. Look up the owners in the county property records and call or write them to ask whether they'd be interested in selling. If the house is in desperate need of a paint job or has a severely overgrown lawn, you may have found motivated sellers before they've actually put the property on the market. If they want to sell, you may have found a property at a very good price.

2. *The garage sale.* Sometimes, before owners put their property up for sale, they'll hold a garage sale to clear the house of all clutter and get it into showing shape. So keep an eye on your local paper for garage sales and moving sales in your target area. Don't waste time attending the sales. Just call to find out what they're selling. During the conversation, explain that you're looking for a home in the area—and ask the person

with whom you're speaking whether the owners know of any that are coming up for sale. Occasionally, you may find that you can buy not only what's in the garage, but also the house itself.

3. *Out-of-state owners.* Whenever you're researching local property values, be sure to make note of all out-of-state property owners. The property rolls should list the mailing address of each owner, in addition to the details of the property itself. When owners' have out-of-state addresses, send them a letter or look them up in the phone directory and call them to find out whether they might be interested in selling.

4. *Code violations.* A property with a number of code violations can be a signal that the owner cannot afford to keep the property up or may no longer be interested in taking care of it. Some towns will physically tag a property that has code violations. Learn to recognize that tag and keep an eye out for it as you drive through your target area.

ALWAYS HAVE A PLAN B

The most important principle in reducing risk and increasing your profit potential on every property flip is to have a solid backup plan in place. Even though you may have no plans to rent out a property you intend to flip, it's best to make sure you *could* rent it out at a profit (or at least break even) if you had to.

Go into every real estate deal—whether you're planning on flipping or investing for the long term—with a good defense. And your best defense is to make sure the rental income the property would produce will cover your carrying costs plus at least 10 percent . . . just in case.

To determine your margin of safety on a particular property, calculate the *gross rental yield*. To do that, divide the rental income it would bring in each year by the asking price. So if the asking price for a home is $100,000 and the rental income is $750 per month, the gross rental yield would be 9 percent ($750 times 12 = $9,000; $9,000 divided by $100,000 = .09).

In most markets, a 10 percent rental yield provides a comfortable margin of safety. In other words, in the worst-case scenario, if the property does not sell, you could rent it out and more than cover your costs.

START LEARNING MORE ABOUT
REAL ESTATE NOW!

If you want to get going, you'll need a lot more information than I've given you here. Fortunately, there are reams of advice about real estate at your local library. If you want to really accelerate your learning curve, I recommend ETR's real estate course.

CHAPTER 8

―――

INVESTING IN THE STOCK MARKET— THE SMART WAY

Most financial planning books devote the bulk of their paper to talking about portfolio management and taxes. I'm going to cover both of those topics in this short chapter.

I don't have a lot to say for two reasons:

1. I'm not a financial planner. I'm a businessman.
2. I believe that you don't need to be an expert in stock investing or taxes to become wealthy—and what you should know about those subjects to grow your wealth can be explained pretty briefly.

In my previous book, the best-selling *Automatic Wealth: The Six Steps to Financial Independence* (Wiley, 2005), I sustained some criticism for giving short shrift to stocks, insurance, and taxes. Not surprisingly, most of the critics were financial planners and brokers—people who make their living by selling stocks, insurance, and tax advice. And most of them never figured out how to become wealthy themselves.

It comes down to this. Books on wealth can be divided into two categories: those written by businesspeople who had no formal education in finance but became wealthy anyway (think J.P. Getty and Donald Trump) and those written by formally educated financial planners and economists, such as my aforementioned critics. I like to count myself among the un-educated group.

Having gotten that out of my system, let me summarize what I think you need to know about stock investing and taxes.

- *About stock investing:* It's very hard to beat the market. Unless you think you might be interested in stock invest-ing as an intellectual challenge, I'd recommend you be content with compounded 10 percent to 13 percent gains. (I'll tell you how to do that in a bit.)
- *About taxes:* It's impossible to beat the tax man. Since the implementation of 1982's Tax Equity and Fiscal Respon-sibility Act, there have been no tax shelters worth pursu-ing (although there are plenty of insurance brokers and financial planners who will sell you plans that pretend to do just that). The only two substantial tax benefits worth your attention come from owning real estate and having your own business. We'll talk about that later.

THE SKINNY ON THE STOCK MARKET

I said I wasn't an expert on the stock market. I'm not. But I've been a consultant to the investment advisory industry for more than 20 years—and during that time, I've seen a lot of investment seminars and heard a heap of speeches about getting rich through stock investing.

There are as many investment experts on the stock market today as there are pages of the *Wall Street Journal*. Studies prove that most of these experts—the great majority of them—never beat the averages. By "averages," I mean the indexes that track major markets.

Some stock experts do beat the market. But most of them do so only for relatively short periods of time. If you had a list of the top-performing stock gurus or fund managers for 2005, for example, it wouldn't be a good indicator of who will be at the top of the list in 2006. Short-term results are not—as the SEC keeps reminding us—reliable.

Experts and funds that have longer-term, above-market track records are rare, but they do exist. If you like the idea of beating the market and you are very disciplined in your financial habits, locating and investing in such a fund or with such an expert might get you above-market rates. And if you go back to Chapter 2, you will see the difference between how much wealth you can accumulate, over a long period of time, by getting an 18 percent ROI as compared with, say, a 13 percent or a 10 percent return.

If you like the idea of beating the market, there are several services that can point you toward funds and/or experts with great long-term track records. Be forewarned, however: Most investors who take this route end up with results that are lower than those of the funds and/or experts they are invested in/with. How can this be? The answer to that is an important lesson in human psychology, one that is so critical to your future wealth that it justifies a short explanation.

Dr. Van K. Tharp is a stock analyst who is on the advisory board of the Oxford Club (an investment group I highly recommend, by the way). He argues that even smart people make the wrong investment choices, because to some degree we are all motivated by the cardinal sins of the investing world: fear, greed, insecurity, and laziness.

"Most people, when they are investing, simply follow their own natural inclinations, and, in doing so, they feel that they are avoiding risk," says Tharp in "Two Ways to Reduce Investment Risks," (*Early to Rise* #558, April 19, 2002). "These natural inclinations often lead them to heavy losses."

People's "natural inclinations" usually peak at a time when the market seems to be turning against them. Fear and greed kick in, and the tendency is to abandon sensible investing programs and jump on whatever trend happens to be hot.

Insecurity—a sin of the ego—makes it difficult for investors to admit that they were wrong about a stock they put their money into. Not admitting you were wrong means not selling a bad stock when it's going down. Many investors never sell their stocks, even when they are left with pennies on the dollar. A healthy attitude about investing is one that says, "Although I invested in this stock in good faith, I'll never know enough about the stock or the market generally to be 100 percent right all of the time. When the market causes a particular stock price to come down, that is just its way of telling me that I didn't have all the facts."

Laziness prevents people from doing the right thing. Or anything at all. They believe it is much easier to sit back and let their stocks play themselves out. Stock prices moving up is not exactly a clarion call to action. Moving down? Also not a time to panic. The worm will turn. Such people think they are being patient. Patience *is* a virtue in investing—especially when applied to the stock of big, established companies that you want to hold on to for 5 to 10 years. But patience should not be confused with running on empty out of sheer laziness.

So much for the four deadly sins of stock investors.

THE *HULBERT FINANCIAL* DIGEST

Of the hundreds of investment advisers that I know and have worked with, there are very few I could actually recommend to you. Not because they aren't (sometimes) very hot. Not because they aren't honest (some of them being honest to a fault). And not because they don't know what they are doing.

It's just that, over the long run, I've seen even the best of them blow hot and cold when it comes to picking stocks.

That's where the *Hulbert Financial Digest* (*HFD*) comes in.

Created in 1980, Mark Hulbert's *Financial Digest* is a monthly newsletter that presents an unbiased rating system of more than 180 stock and mutual fund investment letters. *HFD* uses facts—rather than unsubstantiated claims—to show the actual performance of the 500-plus portfolios recommended by the various newsletters.

Examining the performance records of each stock and mutual fund investment letter—going as far back as 1980—will help you determine which newsletter's advice is most likely to consistently make you money.

You can sign up for the *HFD* online through MarketWatch.com.

If you want to be successful as a stock investor, you must have these three virtues:

1. *Modesty.* You don't need to be the best and most successful investor in the world. If you set modest objectives—10 percent to 15 percent—you will have a good chance of reaching them.
2. *Humility.* You don't know enough to predict the

future. Admit it by setting stop-loss points and sticking to them. (I'll have more to say about this in a minute.)
3. *Consistency.* Umpteen studies have shown that the most important factor in stock market success is the consistent application of a rational system. Which system you follow is not as important as your consistency in adhering to it.

A 10 percent to 15 percent ROI may not make you wealthy overnight. But if you stick to these three virtues—and don't abandon them when you hear an irresistible story about a "can't lose" stock—chances are you will do much better than your friends and colleagues.

USING RANKINGS TO FORM AN INVESTMENT SYSTEM

Table 8.1, compiled from Morningstar.com, lists the 10 no-load mutual funds with the highest rates of return over the last 10 years. Including some of these funds in your portfolio should give you consistently high rates of return. If you have the mental discipline to stick unflinchingly to one proven system, this is an option for you.

If you take this option, I have one specific recommendation regarding the sort of stock-selection system you should choose. Select a system or guru that believes in limiting losses by setting stop-loss points.

PLANNING YOUR EXIT STRATEGY

The hardest part of investing is knowing when to sell. When you're in the thick of things, you may find yourself wanting to

TABLE 8.1

The Top 10 No-Load Mutual Funds,
Ranked by a 10-Year Rate of Return

Ticker	Mutual Fund	10-Year Rate of Return
WMICX	Wasatch Micro Cap	24.15%
BRUSX	Bridgeway Ultra-Small Company	23.60%
GMCDX	GMO Emerging Country Debt III	21.95%
BRAGX	Bridgeway Aggressive Investors 1	21.88%
CGMRX	CGM Realty	21.40%
FIMPX	First American Small Cap Growth Opp Y	21.13%
EUEYX	Alpine U.S. Real Estate Equity Y	20.38%
BRUFX	Bruce Fund	20.36%
MVALX	Meridian Value	19.44%
FSTEX	AIM Energy Inv	19.24%

Source: Data from Morningstar.com.

hang on to what you have, even as the market marches slowly down, taking your investment with it. That's why it is so important to plan your exit strategy *before* you invest.

Investment expert Steve Sjuggerud recommends a *trailing-stop-loss* strategy to prevent your investments from bottoming out. This strategy uses the *25 percent rule,* meaning that you should sell a stock when it has fallen 25 percent from its highest price since you've owned it—no matter what. Let's look at two examples of when a trailing-stop strategy would take effect:

1. You buy a stock at $50 a share. The stock immediately begins to fall. With your trailing-stop strategy, you would automatically sell when the stock reaches $37.50—25 percent less than the amount you invested.

183

2. You buy another stock at $25. This stock rises steeply until it is worth $75 but then begins to fall. Your trailing-stop strategy would have you sell when the stock reaches $56.25—25 percent less than the highest value of the stock.

This type of exit strategy works because (1) it is much better to lose small amounts of money than to lose larger amounts, and (2) it limits premature selling, allowing your better stocks to rise freely.

The problem with stop-losses is that they sometimes take you out of an investment that later on goes back up. And if you have only a small amount of money to invest and it's being stopped out all the time, your capital will eventually be eroded away to nothing.

The problem here isn't the stock-selling strategy itself. It's a lack of capital. And if you have only $10,000 to invest, you are not going to get rich on it no matter what strategy you use. So you have to increase your investment base. (As I said before, you can invest more money only if you have more money to invest—and having more money is a matter of making more and spending less.)

HOW TO REDUCE YOUR RISK

The reason I like stop-losses is simple: The stock market is not a fixed game that can be figured out; rather, it is a dynamic universe, the laws of which can only be guessed at.

There are many factors that go into the movement of the market generally, without my even mentioning the action on any individual stock. Not just the dozens of factors that stock analysts often talk about (momentum, volume, interest rates, etc.) but hundreds of other economic, financial, political, and social factors . . . not to mention the effect of thousands of business-related events and millions of individual investor decisions. The stock market is composed of billions of specific actions and decisions that affect each other but are not necessarily related and are definitely not predictable.

However clever the system seems, however smart the experts, there is simply no way to do what they are trying to do: predict the future of stocks on a consistent basis. The best systems will inevitably fail now and then.

A stock system that accounts for that inevitable failure is a smart system. I'm talking about a system that says, in effect, "Gee, that share price didn't go where I thought it would. I guess something I didn't know about must have happened." Dr. Tharp offers two techniques for a smart system that will reduce the risk of any investment.

> *Technique 1. Diversify over time.* One of the best ways to reduce your risk is to diversify over time. This means that you must always keep enough money in reserve for those special trades that occasionally come along, or even for routine trades during entirely different market conditions. This is also referred to as reducing your "exposure" to risk. As Tharp explains, "If you win 90 percent of the time but risk much of what you have every time you trade, you will eventually lose everything. This is one of the common mistakes of small and novice traders."
>
> *Technique 2: Diversify your account.* If you open several simultaneous positions, trade only independent, low-risk stocks. If your positions are independent, three different positions might be enough to diversify adequately. When one position goes down, another independent position might go up and thereby pro-

vide you with some protection. Most people don't understand diversification. The stocks of two international oil companies, for example, are not independent, because their prices will tend to move together. ("Two Ways to Reduce Investment Risk," *Early to Rise* #558, April 19, 2000.)

Having said all that, I should tell you that I have never, myself, tried to outsmart the market. Let me correct that: Early in my investing career, I invested in individual stocks and individual stock-selection systems several times. I never made any money. The reason was that I didn't really understand the stocks, nor did I care whether the people recommending them had good long-term track records. If a stock story sounded great, I took it. This is the worst way to invest: with your heart.

Lacking the discipline to invest with my mind, I have made it a policy to be satisfied with achieving market averages. In recent years, this has meant a return on investment of 5 percent to 15 percent. Since I'm not investing for the short term, I'm more than happy to get the 10 percent to 13 percent ROIs that the markets have been giving for the past 100-year and 50-year cycles.

And that's what I'd encourage you to do: Forget about trying to do better than the market. Focus your attention instead on increasing your income and investing the lion's share of that extra money in a combination of stocks, real estate, and your own business. You'll do much better in the long run with real estate and entrepreneurship, I believe, because those investments are likely to give you ROIs of 30 percent to 50 percent or even more—and with less actual risk than you'll find in the stock market.

Why is that the case?

For two reasons, both of which I alluded to earlier:

1. *Knowledge:* You are likely to know much more about your own business and your local housing market than about somebody else's public company.
2. *Leverage:* Because your knowledge is greater, your risk is lower. Because your risk is lower, it is more feasible to take advantage of leverage by borrowing the capital you need. Borrowing to invest in your own business (after you have proven to yourself that it works) is a relatively risk-free transaction. The same can be said for mortgaging good properties in your local area.

That explains why I tend to be such a conservative stock investor. I know I'll make loads of money by focusing on my businesses and my real estate holdings, so I'm happy to get a return of between 10 percent and 13 percent by taking a low-risk position in stocks.

How do I get those no-hassle long-term 10 percent to 13 percent returns? By putting some of my money in what are called *index funds.* Index funds are mutual funds that are invested in such a wide variety of companies that they tend to perform at the same rate as the part of the market they track. There are index funds that track the Dow, the S&P 500, and several other major indexes.

Index funds (and exchange-traded funds, or ETFs) have outperformed individually managed portfolios time and time again. In *Double Your Retirement Income* (Wiley, 2005), financial expert Peter Mazonas explains why:

1. "Eight out of 10 actively managed mutual funds neither equal nor outperform the index they strive to match. Professional money managers trade against each other in an efficient market in which the sum of their daily activity establishes the price of each respective index. They underperform the indexes by almost 3 percent on

average, or approximately twice their 1.5 percent average annual management fee." (p. 139)

2. "Buying and holding index funds or exchange-traded funds will save you a minimum of 3 percent annually in lower management fees and trading costs. In this way you will approximate the market indexes, thus beating most of the pros." (p. 139)

3. "Individual investors often buy and sell for all the wrong reasons and usually at the wrong time. To make a trade there must be a buyer and a seller—you versus the professionals. They profit from your mistakes while they cannot even beat the indexes." (p. 145)

Buying index funds may seem too simple a strategy to take seriously. But Warren Buffett, probably the greatest individual investor of all time, had this to say about it:

Most investors . . . will find that the best way to own common stocks is through an index fund that charges minimal fees. Those following this path are sure to beat the net results (after fees and expenses) by the great majority of investment professionals. (From chairmen's letter to Berkshire Hathaway Shareholders, February 29, 1997, at www.ifa.com, January 2006.)

Peter Lynch, the legendary manager of the Fidelity Magellan Fund (once the largest mutual fund) agrees:

Most investors would be better off in an index fund rather than investing in an actively managed equity mutual fund. (*Barron's*, April 2, 1990, p. 15.)

The managers of the biggest investment funds understand that this is true. That's why pensions and endowments are 43 percent invested in index funds.

So how come you don't see index funds recommended in newspapers, magazines, and on television?

Consider this: Brokerage firms spend billions of dollars every year on advertising. Why do they have so much money to spend on it? Because they make so much money on the fees, commissions, and other charges for managing customer accounts. Investing through a traditionally structured brokerage is not cheap. Of course, brokerages don't want you to realize that.

If you have ever invested in an annuity, an insurance policy, or stocks, you've noticed that it's hard to figure out exactly how much you are being charged to service your account. Despite federal regulations to 'fess up, banks, 401(k) providers, brokerage firms, and insurance companies display enormous talent when it comes to keeping their customers confused about fees.

The average actively traded stock fund charges 1.5 percent annually for management. But there are all sorts of extra "transaction fees," commissions, and "research" charges that are not clearly stated in the sales literature but are nonetheless charged to your account. Added up, the total cost to you can be as high as 10 percent in the first year.

Mazonas gives this example: Suppose a broker convinced you to invest $10,000 in a typical, high-fee family of mutual funds. In addition to the 1.5 percent management fee that you would be aware of, you would also be charged the following additional fees:

Sales commission to buy the fund	6%	$600
Cost to execute trades each year	1.5%	$150
12(b)(1) advert. and deferred commission	0.75%	$75

In other words, the $10,000 you invested would be chopped down by $975. Instead of having $10,000 in action, you'd start off with only $9,025.

According to Mazonas:

Not all of these costs are involved in the transaction, either as up-front fees or as redemption charges when you sell the mutual funds. [But] if all these typical costs were charged, you would have to make a 9.75 percent rate of return ($975) the first year just to stay even with the day you [invested]. After paying those first-year fees and commissions, you are left with $9,025. But you are still going to be overpaying in fees each year by 2 percent, even if you make no trades. After fees and front-end charges, assuming a pre-fee 8 percent annual return, at the end of 35 years your $9,025 will grow to $51,700 in inflation-adjusted "today's" dollars. By contrast, had you bought $10,000 of the no-load Vanguard 500 Index Fund with its 0.18 percent management fee, which holds a weighted average of the stocks that make up the Standard & Poor's 500 Index, your money would have grown to $138,818 at the same assumed pre-fee 8 percent annual return. The difference is in the costs over the 35-year period, plus the first-year commissions. (*Double Your Retirement Income,* pp. 142, 143.) (See Table 8.2.)

Today, you can find funds that charge you even less than 0.18 percent. Both Fidelity Investments and the Vanguard

TABLE 8.2

Accumulation of Fees in Vanguard Index versus Average Stock Fund

Investment	Management Fee	Total 35-Year Fees
Vanguard 500 Index	0.18%	$9,035
Average stock fund	1.51%	$61,046

Group have reduced many of their funds (for larger accounts usually, starting at $100,000) to only 0.10 percent.

As Mazonas puts it:

> It is much easier to decide to buy index funds or exchange-traded funds that have 2 percent lower fees and trading costs than to play the market and try to squeeze out a 2 percent higher annual investment yield. Depending on the market, a 2 percent greater yield means you have to make a 20 percent or 25 percent higher rate of return. (*Double Your Retirement Income*, p. 143.)

THE MAJOR MARKET INDEXES

While there are multitudes of specialized indexes, we are going to concentrate on the following seven basic ones; that's because they determine the makeup of the lowest-cost index mutual funds and exchange-traded funds.

Keep in mind that it is difficult to compare performance among the various indexes, because they are made up of different groups of companies.

1. *S&P 500.* Created in 1928, the Standard & Poor's 500 value-weighted index lists 500 stocks traded on the New York Stock Exchange, American Stock Exchange, and Nasdaq National Market. Each company exerts an influence on the performance of the index relative to the market value of that company. The market capitalization of companies in the financial, information technology, and health care industries makes up over half of the index.

(continues)

2. *Nasdaq (National Association of Securities Dealers Automated Quotation System).* Created in 1971, the Nasdaq composite is an index of over 7,200 stocks. It includes all of these stocks that are actively traded, no matter the share value. It is heavily weighted toward technology stocks.

3. *Dow Jones Industrial Average.* Created in 1896, the Dow includes 30 widely traded companies. It is a reliable indicator of both daily market direction and market sensitivity.

4. *Frank Russell Company Indexes.* Over 20 years old, this series of indexes includes the Russell 3000, the Russell 1000, and the Russell 2000.
   - The Russell 3000 is made up of 3,000 actively traded, market-capitalization-weighted companies.
   - The Russell 2000 measures the performance of the bottom 2,000 stock companies that compose the Russell 3000.
   - The Russell 1000 measures the performance of the top 1,000 stock companies that compose the Russell 3000.

5. *Wilshire 5000 Index.* Created in 1974, this index follows the 5,200 most commonly traded U.S. companies (companies headquartered in the United States).

6. *Morgan Stanley Capital International Europe, Australasia, Far East Index.* Created in 1969, the EAFE follows 1,100 equity securities with limited U.S. representation. The index covers stock markets in 24 countries, with major representation from Japan and Europe.

7. *Lehman Aggregate Bond Index.* Created in 1976, this index tracks the market-weighted changes in assorted corporate bond indexes, mortgage-backed securities, and U.S. government bonds.

That's pretty much all I have to say about stock investing. I have even less to say about taxes.

WHAT YOU NEED TO KNOW ABOUT TAXES

The more wealth you build up, the more you will have to pay to the government. That said, you will be able to get some substantial tax breaks on the real estate you're going to invest in and that small business you're going to start. So that's what I'm going to focus on here.

The Tax Advantages of Investment Real Estate

You may not think of it as such, but real estate investing is a business—and taxes are a major expense of that business. If you learn how to minimize taxes, you could substantially increase your profits. Justin Ford of *Main Street Millionaire* lists eight tips for how to reduce the taxes on your investment properties.

1. *Your mortgage interest is deductible.* As a recent grad, you may be unaware that homeowners get a major tax break that is unavailable to renters: Homeowners can deduct their mortgage interest. You may also be able to deduct the mortgage interest on your investment properties. Keep in mind that if you realize a loss on your rental property for tax purposes, you may face certain restrictions when filing for that loss. Check out the section titled "Special Allowance for Rental Real Estate Activities" in the Internal Revenue Service (IRS) instructions for Form 8582 for more information.

2. *All operating expenses are deductible.* Because owning a rental property is a type of business, you are allowed to

deduct all legitimate business expenses against your rental income. Expenses that are deductible include the cost of insurance, management fees, advertising expenses, utilities (those that you, not your tenants, pay), travel expenses to and from the investment property, and one-time fees associated with financing or refinancing (for the survey, home inspection, appraisal, and mortgage discount points). You may also deduct the costs of normal maintenance, such as landscaping and painting. But capital improvements—such as installing a new heating system—are not deductible.

3. *Look into historic preservation exemptions.* If you own property that has been designated as a town landmark or a historical monument, you may be eligible for an exemption for tax increases due to property improvements. For more information on special tax breaks that might be available to you, contact your local tax assessor and your community development board.

4. *Save by closing early in the year.* Most tax authorities reassess properties annually, either on a calendar-year or a fiscal-year basis. When a tax authority's year begins, it reassesses properties that sold during the previous year. This means that if you close on a property in January of 2005, it may not be reassessed until January of 2006. Therefore, throughout 2005, you pay taxes based on the old assessed value of the property. Beginning in 2006, you will be assessed based on the new market value of the property. By closing in January, then, you may save thousands of dollars for the first year you own the property. It won't be until January of 2006 that it will be reassessed at the higher market value.

When you spot a good property at a good price, you should grab it regardless of when you'll have to close on it. But if you're buying near the end of the tax assessment year, see if you can push the closing back a few weeks to the beginning of the new year. You just may buy yourself a "partial tax holiday" for close to a year—and save yourself a few thousand dollars in the process.

5. *Do you qualify for special exemptions?* For a homeowner and investor, there are other ways to save on property taxes. For instance, many states offer homeowners who are disabled or widowed or who are military veterans additional exemptions. These special exemptions are small, saving you perhaps $100 a year. But you might as well claim them if you're entitled to them.

   There are additional exemptions—sometimes amounting to a 100 percent exemption from property taxes—for properties owned by charitable and religious organizations. Check with your local tax authority to see if any of these special tax-reduction programs might apply to you.

6. *Take tax breaks for restoring run-down historic buildings.* On the investment side, you may find tax break programs—often in historic districts or in blighted neighborhoods targeted for redevelopment. And the savings offered in these cases can be very substantial. Your state and the federal government may have tax incentive programs for property owners who restore historic buildings in designated historic areas. And you may be able to dramatically reduce the restoration costs of a building with state and federal income tax rebates. You not only can get some beautiful old buildings at very low prices per square foot but also find that the government is willing to subsidize your repair costs.

7. *Use your IRA to save you money.* When you're just starting out, this may not be a viable option. But once

you've increased your income and have put a hefty chunk into your retirement fund, you might want to consider using your IRA to purchase investment properties. You can save a great deal of money in the process. Your IRA or qualified retirement plan can buy single-family homes, multiunit properties, commercial property, and apartment complexes. It can even buy a distressed or foreclosed property at auction. Your IRA can also borrow to finance the purchase.

If you're self-employed and make a good deal of money, you could deduct as much as $40,000 (or 25 percent of your gross adjusted income, whichever is less) off your current year's income by putting that money in your SEP-IRA and using it as a down payment for a property.

Once your IRA buys a property, all net rental income is tax deferred. And you can sell properties while deferring all taxes on the gains as well. You'll pay taxes only when you distribute IRA gains when you retire. If you own the property in a Roth IRA, the income and the gains are tax free (even when ultimately distributed) because you funded the Roth with after-tax dollars.

8. *Defer capital gains with a like-kind exchange.* Even with properties you buy and sell outside of a retirement plan, you can defer capital gains taxes indefinitely. The key is to use a little-known provision of the IRS Code—Section 1031—which allows for tax-deferred "like-kind exchanges." You buy a rental property and begin to depreciate it. The property could double in value, and with a 1031 like-kind exchange you could still trade it for a rental property of equal or greater value without incurring taxes. You don't need to

negotiate a direct trade to take advantage of this. You can do it on virtually any two (or more) rental properties, as long as you have a qualified intermediary to purchase the properties for you.

Properties that qualify for a Section 1031 like-kind exchange "must be held by you for investment or for productive use in your trade or business," according to the IRS. They also have to be of "the same nature or character." But they don't have to be exactly the same. Under like-kind regulations, you can sell a single-family-home investment property and buy a 12-unit apartment building. You can also exchange residential for commercial property, and vice versa. You can even sell vacant land and buy "improved land" (that is, land with a building or structure on it). ("Boosting Your Returns Through Shrewd Tax Strategies in Real Estate," Tutorial #14.)

The Tax Advantages of Your Small Business

To reduce your company's taxable profit, you must keep an eye on all business expenses that you can use as tax deductions. Keep in mind that there are very specific rules about what you may and may not deduct.

Here is what the IRS has to say on the subject (Publication 334, Tax Guide for Small Businesses, Section 8, 2005, at www.irs.gov): "To be deductible, a business expense must be both ordinary and necessary. An ordinary expense is one that is common and accepted in your industry. A necessary expense is one that is helpful and appropriate for your trade or business. An expense does not have to be indispensable to be considered necessary."

There are many "ordinary and necessary" expenses of doing business. Here are 13 that just might save you money.

INTERNET DATING . . . WITH A TWIST

In this world of fast food and high-speed Internet, traditional dating can seem slow, painstaking, and even boring. In 2001, 27-year-old Ken Deckinger and his 25-year-old friend Adele Testani took advantage of this by founding Hurry Brands, LLC, which offers a high-speed Internet dating service known as HurryDate.

HurryDate gives clients the opportunity to have up to 25 four-minute "mini-dates" a night. They evaluate each date in order to decide whether to pursue a second—and hopefully longer—meeting with the same person.

Deckinger says that the best thing about running HurryDate is that "we are having a positive impact on the lives of tons and tons of people. We are producing a product that makes people happy." In fact, HurryDaters—the company's term for its clients—sometimes end up falling in love, marrying, and having children.

Among perseverance and "dedication to making the business successful," Deckinger credits his youth as crucial to its success. "Everything we were doing was within our demographic," he explains. Instead of being a disadvantage to the business, his and Testani's youth was "a benefit, because it allowed us to relate to our customers." Deckinger admits, however, that "there is something to be said for experience. And experience comes with age."

As someone who has seen his share of business failures as well as successes, Deckinger cautions young entrepreneurs to "follow your passions [and] don't give up, but listen to people who are experienced."

Founded in 2001, HurryDate began in only 10 cities. Even then, its projected earnings were well over $500,000. It has since branched out all over the United States, Great Britain, and Canada, hosting "date parties" in 50 cities all over the country. It has hosted over two million mini-dates since its inception.

Source: Nichole L. Torres, "All in the Family," *Entrepreneur*, April 2002.

1. *Education expenses.* You may be able to deduct the cost of education if you are going to school to maintain or improve skills essential to your business. Don't try to deduct your undergraduate or graduate education expenses, though. Those costs don't usually count.

2. *Expenses of going into business.* While you won't be able to deduct the expenses of getting your business up and running, you can deduct those bills (office rent, utilities, repairs, etc.) that you get after you make your first sale.

3. *Advertising and promotion expenses.* You may deduct the cost of ordinary advertising, such as business cards, newspaper and Yellow Pages ads, and promotional mailings. You may also be able to deduct the cost of promotional advertising that creates business good-will—sponsoring a sports team, for example—if there is a clear relationship between your business and the sponsorship.

4. *Moving expenses.* To qualify for deductions of certain moving expenses, you must be able to prove that the move is the direct result of your business.

5. *Legal and professional fees.* You may be able to deduct the cost of hiring lawyers, tax professionals, or consul-

PATIENCE CAN PAY OFF

If you sell a property within a year, you'll pay income taxes on your gains—which currently can range up to 35 percent. Justin Ford reminds us that if you sell a property you've held for longer than a year you'll be able to pay the long-term capital gains tax, currently 15 percent. He gives us this quick example:

If you've got $50,000 in quick-flip profits staring you in the face after six months, you might want to wait another six months and a day before selling. If you can get the same $50,000 in gains, you could save as much as $12,500 in taxes. And that's just for starters. Depending on your state income and capital gains taxes, you can save a few more thousand dollars there too.

And what if you're in the 15 percent tax bracket? If you flipped for a quick $20,000 profit and your tax bracket is 15 percent . . . would it matter if you pay that 15 percent in capital gains taxes or income taxes?

The answer: It matters. If you're in the 10 percent to 15 percent tax bracket, your long-term capital gains rates are just 5 percent. So a $20,000 profit on a quick flip might result in $3,000 in short-term capital gains taxes (at 15 percent). But long-term capital gains on the same profit would be just $1,000 (5 percent of $20,000).

Source: "Boosting Your Returns through Shrewd Tax Strategies in Real Estate," Tutorial #14, *Main Street Millionaire.*

tants. If the work they do for you relates to a future time, you will be able to make deductions over the lifetime of the benefit.

6. *Auto expenses.* If you use your vehicle for business purposes, or if your business owns its own vehicle, you may

ROUTINE BUSINESS DEDUCTIONS

Don't forget these common expenses you may be able to list as deductions:

- Bank fees on business accounts
- Business association dues
- Business cards and stationery
- Business-related entertainment
- Casual labor and tips
- Casualty and theft losses
- Commissions and fees
- Consultant fees
- Contributions to a retirement fund
- Credit bureau fees
- Depreciation of business property
- Gifts to customer or suppliers
- Insurance
- Licenses and regulatory fees
- Mileage for business travel
- Office supplies
- Online computer services
- Parking
- Postage
- Promotion and publicity
- Software
- Subscription to trade publications
- Taxi and bus fare
- Telephone calls while traveling

deduct certain operation and maintenance costs. If you use the vehicle for both business and personal purposes, you can deduct only the cost of business usage.

7. *New equipment.* You may either write off the full cost of certain business assets or deduct their cost over a number of years. Real estate, inventory marked for resale, and property purchased from a close relative do not qualify for deductions.

8. *Improvements.* You can deduct the cost of repairs that maintain the normally efficient operating condition of a business asset. You may not, however, deduct improvements that increase the value of the asset, lengthen the time you can use the asset, or make it adaptable to a different use.

9. *Bad debt.* If your business sells goods, you may deduct the cost of any goods that are sold but not paid for. Services that are provided but not paid for do not qualify for deductions.

10. *Travel expenses.* Business travel expenses—including airfare, operation of a vehicle or use of other transportation, lodging, meals, shipping business materials, clothes laundering, telephone calls, faxes, and tips—are deductible. You may take deductions only for your own expenses, not for those of a person you're traveling with.

11. *Business entertaining.* If you entertain a business prospect or customer, you may deduct half the cost of entertainment if it is directly related to the business, if business is discussed, or if it occurs immediately before or after a business meeting.

12. *Interest.* You may deduct the interest and carrying charges on business purchases. You may also deduct the interest on personal loans put toward your business.

13. *Taxes.* Sales tax on ordinary business purchases, excise and fuel tax, and real estate tax are all deductible. As for the other taxes: Self-employment tax is paid by an individual and isn't deductible as a business expense. State income tax is deducted on your personal return as an itemized reduction rather than as a business expense. Federal income tax paid on business income is never deductible.

CHAPTER 9

LIVING RICH
STARTING
TOMORROW

Let's stop for a moment to consider what we've learned so far and how you can benefit from it.

If you follow the suggestions about saving made in Chapter 2 and the investing recommendations made in Chapter 8, you'll be a wealthy person when you and the rest of your graduating class are thinking about retirement.

If you get a good job (as a result of what you learned in Chapters 3 and 4) and follow the guidelines in Chapter 5 about accelerating your income, financial independence will come to you at least 5 or 10 years before retirement.

Investing in real estate (as described in Chapter 7) will accelerate that process. And if you start your own business and put into practice the business-building techniques outlined in Chapter 6, you could very well become wealthy in the next 7 to 10 years—or even sooner. (Several people who have followed the Automatic Wealth program became multimillionaires in fewer than five years.)

The rate at which you implement the Automatic Wealth strategy will determine how soon you become wealthy. Getting rich in 10 years or less will require a simultaneous strong start on all fronts—increasing your income and investing at least 15 percent of it in stocks, real estate, and a side business. If you decide to take a more leisurely path, wealth will take a little longer.

Regardless of the pace you set, there is no reason to feel as if you are depriving yourself along the way. As I'll explain in this chapter, the best things in life—including the material comforts—can be enjoyed by anyone with a reasonably good income, the self-discipline to ignore the lure of brand names, and the wisdom to spend money smartly.

So let's see how you can live a full, rich, and rewarding life while on your way to wealth—long before you've saved enough money to stop working and sail off into the sunset.

HOW TO LIVE A RICH AND WELL-BALANCED LIFE

But first, I have to admit something. I'm not an expert on living a well-balanced life. Everything I told you about getting a good job and making lots of money came from my personal experience. I did it. I did it again and again, and then I helped other people do it. One day I woke up and realized I'd become sort of an expert at getting rich.

But living well? My track record there is spotty. Yes, I've enjoyed all the wonderful things money can buy—the beautiful homes, expensive cars, luxury vacations, private schools for my kids, and privilege. But I learned (as I was told I would) that those sorts of things aren't all they are cracked up to be.

I made all the typical mistakes that are so common with zealous people. I was a demanding boss—sometimes too demanding and I relegated other interests (family and friends, to name just two) to secondary slots. This was a mistake that did not go unpunished. Happily, I never screwed up so badly that I lost those things that matter most . . . but I could have.

I used to rationalize my single-mindedness by arguing that I couldn't have achieved what I did, in terms of business accomplishments and personal wealth, without making getting rich such a strong priority. And there is some truth to that. But only *some* truth. The rest of the truth has come to me over the years in moments of personal reflection—small interpersonal discoveries about how I could have behaved, what I could have said, and when I could have stopped working.

I've developed some ideas about how to accomplish what you want in life without neglecting your family, friends, or personal passions. In this chapter, I'll tell you what I now know about this. It's not advice from an expert, but it has helped me repair some of the damage I've caused . . . and so it might help you avoid causing any similar pain in your life.

With this chapter, my hope is that you will begin to enjoy the best of what wealth has to offer now, even when your wealth is so limited.

SLOW DOWN TO ENJOY LIFE

Einstein proved that time is relative—that it speeds up and slows down in relationship to how fast or slow you are traveling. But psychological time, our perception of its passing, moves faster the older we get.

The natural acceleration of psychological time is enhanced by activity. The more activities we pack into any given period of time, the faster it goes by. A middle-aged person in the midst of a busy career, straddled with the demands of family, friends, and local social obligations, is a psychological freight train blindly rushing forward at 140 miles an hour.

We can't change or even deny the fact that our lives will end. But there are things we can do to decelerate and, as a consequence of slowing down, begin to enjoy all the things that we are meant to enjoy.

For most people the challenge is this: "How do I slow down my life so I can enjoy all of life's riches without giving up on my goal of financial independence?" Or, to put it differently: "How can I get rich without turning into a typical, self-centered, success-addicted workaholic?"

Those are good questions. Here are some answers.

IDENTIFY AND ELIMINATE YOUR MAJOR TIME KILLERS

A time killer is any activity that consumes most or all of your mental energy and provides little—if anything—in the way of lasting benefits. The worst time killers not only give you nothing in exchange for the time you invest in them but also leave you weaker, less energetic, and duller than you were before.

The worst time killers, in my experience, are the following:

- Most TV programming
- All video games
- Web browsing
- At least 70 percent of all e-mail
- Waiting in line without having something productive to do

- Getting angry about waiting in line
- Arguing about anything that will not matter five years later
- Trying to be number one
- Worrying about people stealing your good ideas

The problem is that time killers like television, video games, and Web browsing give you the illusion that you are engaged in a relaxing activity. But what you are really doing is putting your brain and body on hold. Your mental and physical energy levels drop, and that dormant state persists for hours after you discontinue the activity. In other words, you not only waste time while you're watching television but also slow down so much that it's difficult for you to operate at a normal (let alone highly productive) level in the time that follows.

Herbert Krugman is a sociological researcher I remember once reading about, who conducted an experiment with his 20-year-old secretary in 1969. He taped an electrode to the back of her head, flicked on a TV set, and began monitoring her brain waves.

What he found, through repeated trials, was that within about 30 seconds her brain waves switched from predominantly beta waves, indicating alert and conscious attention, to predominantly alpha waves, indicating an unfocused, unreceptive lack of attention—the state of aimless fantasy and daydreaming below the threshold of consciousness.

Many studies have proven that people—from head-injury patients to plain old slackers—who produce an excess of alpha waves have consistently weaker powers of concentration. As you would expect, those who have a great sense of focus have a much higher ratio of beta brain waves.

Eliminating your time killers will give you back hundreds

of precious, productive hours every year—time you can devote to achieving your goals, enjoying friends and family . . . and making the world a little better than you found it.

It's not easy to give up time killers—especially those that are habitual—but it can be done.

One thing that has worked for me is to clear my environment of the time wasters themselves—sort of like clearing the refrigerator of fattening foods. For example, you can eliminate a great deal of your TV watching by unplugging the set and getting rid of the remote control or by eliminating the cable connection so you can use the set only for playing tapes or DVDs.

At our house, for example, the television isn't connected. If a family member wants to watch a show, he or she has to either visit a friend or watch a taped version of it while exercising. When the treadmill stops, so does the TV watching. This not only eliminates impulsive watching and commercials but also is good for the body.

As you remove time killers from your life, schedule productive activities into the time you have freed up. When you do, you'll notice an increase in your energy level. That's because productive work leaves you with more energy than you had when you began it.

That's how you deal with the big time killers.

Then there are the small ones—those that eat up minutes instead of hours of your time, but still leave you feeling like a zombie. Here are some suggestions for things to do when you're early for an appointment . . . or stuck in a line . . . or sitting in a room waiting for a business meeting to start:

- Always have something with you that you can read.
- Keep a small notepad and pencil in your pocket to capture useful ideas.

- Keep a journal to record your best thoughts and observations.

REDUCE THE STRESS IN YOUR LIFE

Wasting your time decreases the quality of your life. But being stressed is even worse. Not only does it affect the quality of your life, but it also shortens it.

If you ask wealthy people what they most want in life, most answers you get will probably have something to do with slowing down and relaxing more. The best way to accomplish such a goal is to identify those things that give you the greatest stress and then eliminate them from your life, one by one.

Here are nine stress-reducing suggestions, some of which were inspired by Ilene Birkwood's *Stress for Success* (Shoreline Press, 1996) and *The Working Woman's Guide to Managing Stress* (Prentice Hall, 1994) by J. Robin Powell.

1. *Identify—and make time for—your favorite pastimes.* Make a list of the things you enjoy doing most: flyfishing, listening to music, writing poetry, and so on. Are you taking time to do those things? If not, why not? Remember, balance in life is very important. Taking an occasional break to do something that gives you pleasure will increase your level of happiness and provide you with much-needed stress relief.

2. *Destress your diet.* Lack of proper nourishment accelerates cell degeneration in the brain and creates stress in your body. Good nutrition helps you physiologically deal better with stress. You can build healthy eating habits by following three general rules: (1) Reduce your intake of calories from fat and meat; (2) double

your intake of calories from vegetables, fruits, and whole grains; and (3) lower the amount of meat you eat while adding more fish or vegetable protein, such as nuts, peas, beans, and lentils.

3. *Exercise.* Exercise can truly relax you. So make it your goal to exercise at least three times a week by doing something you enjoy. This is important; if you enjoy the activity, you'll be more likely to make it a habit. Another consideration: Choose an exercise that is invigorating and doesn't add to your stress. Even if you love racquetball, for instance, it may be a bad choice for you because it is such an intense (and therefore exhausting) game.

   My advice is to do yoga every morning for 15 minutes—and then another 15 minutes of exercise later in the day. That's all you need to be flexible and fit, and to feel good.

   It's also good to have a physical hobby—a sport like tennis or jiujitsu that you enjoy at least once a week. But don't count that as exercise, because it's not. It's fun.

4. *Get a* restful *night's sleep.* Lack of sleep (or lack of restful, non-REM sleep) can add to your stress. Doing something relaxing before bedtime—maybe listening to soothing music or taking a bath—will help you fall asleep and sleep deeply and restfully. It also helps to give yourself plenty of time to digest a heavy meal and to avoid alcohol, arguments, and any stimulating mental or physical activity before bedtime.

5. *Take regular work breaks.* When you feel particularly stressed at work, take a short break. In fact, don't wait for that to happen. At least once an hour, get up from your chair and walk around your office or down the

hall—maybe even take a little trip outside. Get a glass of water or take a minute to stretch. This will revive you and allow you to approach your work with renewed enthusiasm.

6. *Laugh.* Laughter is one of the best ways to release stress. Regularly expose yourself to things and meet with people that make you laugh.

7. *Have realistic expectations.* Things don't run smoothly 100 percent of the time. People are late for meetings. Traffic slows to a standstill. The person in line in front of you has a credit card that needs to be called in for approval. (That's why you should always be prepared with those little time fillers I recommended.)

8. *Leave your work at work.* If you consistently bring work home with you, you will be a prime candidate for burnout. Reserve your time away from the office for relaxation, recreation, and your family.

9. *Make a big change.* Sometimes you can resolve or eliminate stress only by making a major change. If you feel constantly overwhelmed and anxious at work, perhaps you need to rethink your career goals. Major changes should not, of course, be approached lightly. They may, in fact, cause stress of their own in the short term. But if the long-term benefits could greatly outweigh the immediate stress, it's something to seriously consider.

ONE MORE THING . . .

There's one more technique that can help you slow down and increase your enjoyment of life. It works because it draws from the most fundamental human activity: breathing.

To appreciate how important breathing is to you, put

your head under water and hold your breath for as long as possible. Now consider this: That's how long you could maintain consciousness (even life) without being able to breathe.

So take a full breath right now, and enjoy. Consider how amazing it is that you keep breathing without any conscious effort . . . and that you have been breathing, more or less without interruption, for your entire life. At an average rate of about 12 breaths per minute, that comes to 720 breaths per hour, 17,280 per day, and 6,307,200 per year. That amounts to over a quarter of a billion opportunities to appreciate your life in a 40-year time span!

Promise yourself that you will never again take breathing for granted. In your daily schedule, assign at least a few minutes every morning and every evening to consciously practicing breathing—enjoying the miracle of each inhalation, the relaxation possible with each exhalation.

STOP THINKING ABOUT YOURSELF

When you are stressed, you tend to spend time thinking about your problems. When you spend too much time thinking about yourself, you become unhappy.

Contrary to what many popular self-improvement gurus say, "taking care of number one" is probably the worst way to overcome emotional problems and the best way to speed up your life so that its best moments are lost to you.

There is a relationship between egocentrism and time. That relationship is simply this: The bigger your ego (i.e., the more self-involved you are), the faster time will move for you. Conversely, the more you pay attention to things outside of yourself, the slower time will move for you, enabling you to capture life's best moments.

You can prove this to yourself with a little experiment. The next time you wash your car, do half of it the way you normally would—but while consciously thinking about the many problems and opportunities that are forcing themselves into your life. What you'll probably notice is that the experience is either mildly unpleasant or neutral, but that you have very little awareness of the car itself or the washing of it. Time passes quickly, and when you are done you feel a little bit disappointed and don't know why.

Now wash the other half of the car, this time keeping your mind completely clear of all outside thoughts. The only thing you should allow yourself to think about is the car you are washing. And you shouldn't think about it in any way that goes beyond the actual washing process. Your goal is to stay in the here and now and see how you feel. My bet is that you will notice time slowing down as your enjoyment of the car, and the process of washing it, increases.

That's what you are shooting for in your daily life: quality, focused experience. The kind of attention to what you're doing that both slows down time and increases the fun you can get from it.

WHAT IT TAKES TO BE HAPPY

People who focus on things outside themselves end up leading happier lives. And that's not all we know about what it takes to be happy.

Martin Seligman, in his book *Authentic Happiness* (Free Press, 2002), lists these discoveries:

- People who are happy are usually oriented toward friends and family rather than themselves, and tend to attract good friends.
- People are happiest when they have satisfying and absorbing work.
- Having responsibilities is not the source of unhappiness, and, conversely, not having responsibilities does not automatically result in happiness.
- Selflessness is a source of happiness, but for the giver rather than the receiver. (This, you know.)
- Those who are happy also generally feel a sense of gratitude.

Each person is born with a sort of preprogrammed regulator that determines how much happiness he or she is comfortable with. This genetic predisposition, new studies say, can be counteracted by force of will—just as you can live at a body weight that is different from that which you are programmed to have.

Here are five things you can do right now to become happier:

1. Find work that you value.
2. Stay close to your family and friends.
3. Recognize that you need only a limited amount of wealth to be happy.
4. Stop worrying about taking care of yourself and start taking better care of others.
5. Be thankful for what you have.

You may have noticed that "getting rich" isn't on this list. So while you're working toward financial success, how much attention should you pay to being happy?

THE RELATIONSHIP BETWEEN
HAPPINESS AND SUCCESS

No matter who they are—top-level executives, retirees, or new graduates like you—people asked what they want out of life, predominantly give two answers:

1. To be happy
2. To be successful

Here's the good news about happiness: Unless you have a psychotic imbalance, happiness is not only possible but relatively easy.

The bad news: Being happy doesn't have a whole lot to do with being successful. Studies show that happy people generally have an overly optimistic view of themselves and the future. They tend to think that other people like them more than they actually do. And they are more sanguine about how their life will unfold than they have a rational right to be.

When I think of the happy people I know, they are that way. They want to see the glass as half full—including the glass that reflects their image.

Pessimists, studies show, have a better record of predicting outcomes than optimists do. And they are also more insightful when it comes to understanding how they are seen by others. Yes, pessimists are more realistic; they are also, however, less happy.

What does this mean? If you want to be happy (and you should), do the following:

- Fill your heart with hope.
- Train your mind to think positively.
- Learn to pay attention to others.

As I mentioned earlier, you'll never become happy if you spend your time dwelling on yourself. Forget about your problems, your limitations, and your bad luck. Think about how you can help others. Work to make the world a better place.

OKAY . . . BUT WHAT ABOUT BEING SUCCESSFUL?

That's happiness. Now let's talk about success.

If you want to accomplish your goals—including your goal of being wealthy—maintaining a positive attitude *will not* be enough. Success requires action.

I think it's fair to say that being successful is an 80/20 proposition:

- Eighty percent of success depends on what you do.
- Twenty percent of success depends on how you think.

Although the "how you think" part is less important, it does matter. For if you don't have the right attitude to begin with, you will never be able to get your goals into action. When one is overwhelmed by fear and uncertainty, it's hard to get any project going.

In his very good book *Bull's Eye Investing: Targeting Real Returns in a Smoke and Mirrors Market* (Wiley, 2004), John Mauldin talks about how thoughts and feelings—including overoptimism, overconfidence, conservatism, confirmatory biases, and hindsight—affect the success of investors. He says, "In the world of our ancestors, overconfidence will get you killed. Lack of confidence will mean you sit around and starve. Cautious optimism is the right approach."

It seems to me that this observation can be applied to success in all areas of life. If we are overconfident, we are likely to fail because we get into projects that have little or no chance of succeeding. If we are underconfident, we are likely to fail because we pass up good opportunities when they come to us, fearing we don't have the resources to take advantage of them.

What we need in life is the right blend of confidence and caution—what Mauldin calls "cautious optimism."

ARE YOU INSTINCTIVELY AN OPTIMIST OR A PESSIMIST?

Ask yourself these questions:

1. "Do I confront challenges with (a) anxiety or (b) happiness?"
2. "When making decisions, do I (a) constantly question myself or (b) have confidence in the choices I make?"
3. "When faced with an unsuccessful attempt, do I (a) feel it is a sign of incompetence or (b) suggest a new approach?"
4. "When with friends, family, or colleagues, (a) am I easily agitated or (b) do I enjoy their company?"
5. "When it comes to happiness, do I feel that (a) good things always happen to others or (b) I am happier than most people?"
6. "Do I view change as (a) a setback or (b) an opportunity?"
7. "When dealing with failure, do I (a) view it as permanent, take it personally, and/or feel hopeless or (b) view it as temporary and nonpersonal and as a great learning experience?"
8. "When faced with a difficult situation, do I find that friends and family (a) seek advice elsewhere or (b) come to me for advice?"
9. "Do I feel that (a) if something can go wrong in my life it will or that (b) I am in control of my own life?"

If you have more (a) answers, your glass is half empty; if you have mostly (b) answers, your glass is half full.

HOW DO YOU ACHIEVE CAUTIOUS OPTIMISM?

Here are a few suggestions:

1. *If you are an optimist, curb your enthusiasm.*
   - Don't sign any contracts or agree to any business deals without running them by a trusted lawyer and an accountant beforehand.
   - Don't buy anything expensive on the spot. And don't agree to buy anything on the spot, either. This applies to all significant purchases, including investments in financial instruments, real estate, businesses, and toys.
   - Don't take a job on the spot. If it's perfect and you love it, say, "I'd love to accept this right now because I know it's perfect for me and I'm sure I'll do the job you are expecting me to do. But I promised my spouse (parent, whomever) that I'd speak to her/him first, and I never break my promises. Can I get back to you with a positive response at nine o'clock tomorrow morning?
   - Don't send out "reactive" e-mails on the spot. Wait 24 hours and then either delete or modify the e-mail.
2. *If you are a pessimist, fill your glass a bit more.*
   - Be happy that you have a natural ability to detect the potential problems in every situation. Use that talent to assess the risks and problems inherent in any major venture you undertake.
   - Make it a habit to always say something positive before you say anything negative or even more neutral that may be on your mind. If you think the soup is oversalted, say, for example, "Gee, this soup has a great texture and a perfect temperature. It would be

even better if it were a little less salty." (Note: Try always to avoid the dreaded—and easily detected— "but" signal, as in "The soup was great, but. . . .")

- After you get through writing your daily task list as the first thing you do in the morning, spend 5 or 10 minutes visualizing every task on it. Imagine yourself happily accomplishing the intended objective. Even if you find the job odious and the person you are doing it with repugnant, find some way to imagine actually enjoying the experience. (I'll tell you more in a minute about making out daily task lists.)
- Practice smiling in the mirror. Do this as often as you can stomach it. And then do it some more.
- When talking on the phone, smile. The person on the other end takes cues from the energy in your voice. If you want that person to respond enthusiastically to your ideas, you need to breathe that enthusiasm into the tone of your voice.
- Every time you see people for the first time, greet them with a firm handshake, a smile, and a confident "eye lock."

HOW TO ACCOMPLISH ALL YOUR MOST IMPORTANT GOALS

Whether you're an optimist, a pessimist, or something in between, recognize that whatever your goals are, you'll have a better chance of achieving them if you follow a formal goal-setting program.

So let's set up your program right now. Take out a sheet of paper. Title it "Life's Goals" (if you have no shame) or "Stuff to Do Before I Croak" (if you are afraid someone will see it).

Now make a list of everything you want to accomplish. Everything. Making a lot of money. Writing books. Traveling to Rome. Learning to tap dance. Write till you are done.

Let the list sit for a few hours—even a day. Then narrow it down to your top 10 choices. Then take another rest. Now make another cut. This time, you have to select your top four goals.

Okay, these are your life goals, top priorities, bottom-line objectives.

Now, of the four, pick one that is numero uno. On a separate sheet of paper—or perhaps on an index card—write down your four goals with your number one objective on top. Highlight that one.

Convert those four goals into five-year objectives. For example, let's say one of your life goals is to have a net worth of $10 million. And let's say you want to retire in 10 years. You might make "having a $5 million net worth" your five-year goal.

You are going to use this five-year list to create a one-year list. And you will use the one-year list to create monthly lists. And you will use each monthly list to create weekly lists. And the weekly lists to create daily task lists.

I know. I know. But it works. It really works.

If you make these four goals your priorities, you will almost surely have to sacrifice other, lesser objectives to achieve them. And to make sure you reach your top goal, you may even have to compromise one or more of the other three. But by using this plan, you will definitely achieve that primary goal—and you will have a much better chance of accomplishing the other three than you would ever have had otherwise.

How will you find the time in your already busy schedule to do what you have to do to reach your life goals? It's easy to do so: Wake up—and get to work—earlier. And use that extra time to do the things that matter most in terms of your long-term success.

Every successful businessperson I know (or have read about) gets to work early. It's such a universal trait of accomplished individuals that I'm tempted to say it is a secret for success. "Early to bed and early to rise," Ben Franklin said, "makes a man healthy, wealthy, and wise." I used to think that was propaganda from a Puritan. Now I think it's an observation from a very wise man.

Think of it this way:

Somewhere inside you a fire is burning. It is your core desire—your deepest, truest idea about what you'd like to do and the person you'd like to become. If you can vent that fire, it will give you all the energy, imagination, and boldness you need to make your life full, rich, and satisfying. If you ignore that fire, it will consume everything that is potentially great and good about you. It will burn out your secret hopes, desires, and passions, one at a time, and leave you—as an older person reflecting back on your life—with a cold, charred core.

By getting up early each morning and making those early hours—as well as the rest of your day—more productive, you can make your life into exactly what it should be. What it should be, of course, is different for every person. Only by digging down deep and finding out what really motivates you—by identifying your life goals—can you find the fire that will fuel your future.

HOW TO LIVE LIKE A BILLIONAIRE

When you think about the rich—the really rich—you may find yourself marveling at their . . . well, their money. Consider, for example, Bill Gates, the world's richest man. If you think $10 million is a fortune, consider this: He has 4,000 of those fortunes. If he put his money in $1,000 bills, he'd have 40 million of them! His wealth is so great that the interest on it makes him $30 million richer every month. Bill Gates makes more money every time he takes a nap than most Americans make in 10 years.

But how much better does he live? Sure, he has a huge house. And a yacht. He's probably got a jet, too. But who needs that crap? Really! If you make at least $100,000 a year, you can live as well as Bill Gates does.

Let's start by identifying some of life's basic experiences:

- Sleeping
- Working
- Dressing
- Eating/drinking
- Leisure

Now the purpose of becoming rich—you might think—should be to make each of these experiences as rewarding as possible. And the more money you have, you might reason, the more choices you should have to enable you to do that.

Consider, for example, sleeping. What does a billionaire want out of sleep time? I'd say the same thing you do: blissful, uninterrupted unconsciousness. And what will give you that (besides peace of mind, which you can't buy)? Answer: a great mattress. And how much does the world's best mattress cost? Maybe $1,500. That means you can buy yourself a million-dollar sleep on a billion-dollar mattress for no more than $1,500. If you are making $100,000 a year, you can easily afford it.

You can get rid of that lumpy thing you are sleeping on and find yourself the best mattress you will ever have. Buy it and go to sleep, content that Bill Gates can have it no better.

BUYING YOURSELF THE BEST

You can pay almost any price for anything. After a certain price point, however, you are no longer paying for quality but for prestige.

Consider steak. If you ask someone who knows about beef, you will most likely be told that the quality of a steak is entirely a matter of the quality of the meat you buy—not the skill of the person who cooks it. If you order a New York strip at Ruth's Chris for around $30, you'll be eating the best steak money can buy. If you order the same cut of meat at Le Cirque, you'll pay $75 for it. What's the difference? Just the prestige of the Le Cirque name.

The same thing is true when it comes to your clothing. Beautiful, comfortable clothes are not cheap, but they don't have to cost a fortune. You can either buy a great pair of slacks for $150 or spend 10 times that amount. The difference will be the label on the waistband.

Champagne, anyone? *Consumer Reports* had some wine experts test a variety of champagnes and found that out of the five best, four cost less than $40. Dom Perignon, listed fifth, will set you back $115. Better champagne can be had for only $28.

And it goes on. The point is this: The best material things in life are affordable. They are not cheap—quality never is—but if you buy them selectively and use them with care, you can enjoy a life as materially rich as Bill Gates's on an income that wouldn't get him through lunch.

Here's how you can live rich on a very modest budget.

YOUR DREAM HOUSE

I have lived in both a three-room mud hut in Africa and a 5,000-square-foot mansion—and I can tell you this: The

223

quality of a home has little or nothing to do with how much it costs or how big it is.

Think about the houses you most admire. They are probably *not* huge and flashy. One of my current favorites is a modest, three-bedroom home in Cleveland that has been transformed by the lady who owns it into a lush, luxurious museum of her love of travel, dance, and learning. Every room is a gem. I am completely comfortable and endlessly amused in this rich and interesting place.

Its value? In all the important ways, it's as great as Bill Gates's 40,000-square-foot monstrosity in Seattle—yet this one has a market value of about $150,000.

To make your home one you will enjoy and be proud of, fill it with things that give you pleasure. And in my opinion, collecting is the best way to satisfy the material girl or guy within you. How good is it? Let me count the ways:

1. You can collect whatever you like best. Just about anything.
2. Collecting is an intellectual pleasure. The more you learn about your collection, the better you'll like it.
3. You can enjoy your collection as often as you like.
4. It makes you more interesting to others.
5. It makes you more interested in others.
6. Your collection will never desert you. It will give you a lifetime of pleasure.
7. There is a reasonable chance that your collection will become more valuable in time.

My first collection consisted of beer bottles. I liked beer and figured that saving the bottles was pretty much a no-brainer. Even if I got no pleasure from the collection, I'd certainly enjoy drinking the beer. As it turned out, I also liked the collecting.

Since then, I've begun several other collections. I have a pretty nice collection of Latin American paintings and sculptures, early-twentieth-century European paintings, antique and current cigar lighters, Day of the Dead artifacts, Santos statues, naïve art, and first editions.

No matter what you collect—antique jewelry, cameras, ceramic coffee mugs, ashtrays, or whatever—you will find that there are others out there doing the same thing.

Pick something you like. It might be something that pleases you (such as landscape paintings) or something that has personal meaning to you (model trains, for example, because you've loved them since your first train trip across the country). Avoid collecting what you can't afford (sixteenth-century Italian icons) or what art brokers try to sell you. Your taste will change—and improve—as you gain experience. So start off small and build steadily.

YOUR CAR

I have a friend—a wealthy friend—who loves cars, especially sports cars. He drives a Camaro. Why? Because he says it is as good as a Corvette, a Porsche, or even a Ferrari. Instead of forking over $150,000-plus, he gets his thrills in a car that costs one-sixth that.

What about prestige? Well . . . that's what you have to pay more for. But if you are willing to go the classic route and buy a car with a design that doesn't change every year or so, you can buy yourself prestige at affordable rates. For example, I drive a mint-condition NSX that you couldn't tell from a brand-new one. My car is worth about $30,000. You'd have to pay almost three times that for a new one. The same holds true for older Mercedes and BMW models.

DRESSING LIKE A BILLIONAIRE

What does it cost to dress like the world's richest people? Much less than you think.

If you can forget about brand names and learn about quality, you will save thousands and look better. As with cars, you'll do better by going after a classic look in clothing. That's because you won't have to discard perfectly good items simply because the lapel has changed.

The other big secret of dressing rich is this: Less is more.

Designer Ralph Lauren—a guy who has the money and the access to dress as rich as one can—wears the same thing almost every day: classic-cut jeans and a T-shirt. NBA coach Pat Riley, one of the best-dressed men in America, wears nothing but Armani suits. He has a number of them . . . but nowhere near the number you'd think to look at him.

You can dress beautifully in secondhand clothes. What could be more impressive than a vintage suit, properly tailored, impeccably clean?

There are books on this subject. They all say pretty much the same thing. A few really nice items are much better— more enjoyable for you, more impressive to others—than a huge wardrobe of trendy, ordinary stuff.

Do you want specifics? Get yourself two or three pairs of slacks or skirts. One or two suits or dresses. Two or three pairs of shoes. Buy only what you love.

Make sure your socks are cashmere ($19.50 at Banana Republic) and that your underwear or lingerie is of the finest quality. Use only one cologne or perfume, but love it. Do the same with hair products and cosmetics. The rule is to have much less, but love everything you have.

Buy classic materials. Insist on quality. A few items can be better than many. Simple is better than complex. Understated is better than flashy. If you follow these guidelines, you will have what Bill Gates can afford to have: a very pleasant feeling every time you pull on your shirt or buckle your belt.

EATING LIKE A BILLIONAIRE

Do you want to enjoy a billion-dollar meal? Take a good bottle of wine and a baguette of freshly baked bread, along with some cheese, ham, and butter, and go to the nearest park with a friend or loved one. You need only a knife and a corkscrew—the ones you have in your kitchen are fine—to prepare and serve a truly memorable meal.

Le Cirque? Well, I told you my opinion about that. Still, if there's an expensive restaurant you are dying to try, go ahead and treat yourself, but not too often. As someone who has eaten countless expensive meals, I know how tiring rich food can be. More important, I can remember few expensive meals that surpassed the simple wine-and-cheese lunches my wife and I enjoyed earlier in life when we were lucky enough to have them.

When you eat at home, I suggest making the meal as fine a dining experience as possible. You can make all your meals elegant by following six simple rules:

1. Pay a little extra for the principal element. For breakfast, buy great, freshly roasted coffee—and grind it yourself. For lunch, pay a little more for salmon salad rather than the tuna variety. For dinner, buy free-range poultry or beef.
2. Use your best service. China and silverware that please you should not be saved for special occasions. Make every occasion special by treating it so.

3. Listen to good music. Music is as much a part of a meal as water is a part of swimming. The only time you can justify not having beautiful music playing softly in the background while you're eating is when you are in the mountains or on the beach.

4. Don't read. There is a time for reading, but it is never while you are eating.

5. Eat slowly. Savor every bite.

THE FINEST SILVERWARE MONEY CAN BUY

Shopping for a Christmas present for my wife, I wandered into an antique shop in town that specializes in silver. The proprietor, a genteel, 86-year-old lady from Georgia, showed me this and that—and then, when she sensed I was looking for something very special, took me to the back room and showed me an absolutely beautiful collection of silverware by the Baltimore-based silversmiths Reed & Barton. It was the Francis I design—the finest they ever made. "If you were a millionaire," she said in her seductive southern drawl, "you could not buy a finer set of silverware than this."

It cost me $4,500. Nothing to be sneezed at, but that was for a set of 14 place settings and a lot of serving utensils. A regular full-service set might cost $2,500. Now think of that. You can own the finest silverware that money can buy—and antique silverware at that—for $4,500. Such a set of silverware could last you all your life, give you pleasure and prestige, and make even your ordinary meals elegant. The Queen Mother herself couldn't do better.

I'm thinking about throwing away the rest of my silverware and using only this. That's how much I like it.

6. At some point during the meal, take a moment to think about how lucky you are to be eating so well.

As I said, even those of you who aren't wealthy can treat yourselves to an occasional meal at a fine restaurant. But there are ways to make dining out at "ordinary" places make you feel like a billionaire, too. Here are a few tips:

- *Dine early.* Try to arrive at a restaurant earlier than most people do. The host or hostess may try to dissuade you if the place hasn't opened for dinner yet, but he or she may be convinced to let you in if you claim to be looking only for a glass of wine and a place to sit. Once you have your wine, ask the waiter or waitress for a menu. This is a good time to start a conversation with the waitstaff, as they won't be busy yet—and may, in fact, be eating their own dinner in the back of the restaurant.

   Ask the waitstaff what they're eating (a good way to get them to warm up to you). Who knows—they might get the cook to bring you a plate of samples (something that rarely happens when a place is full of dinner customers). After checking out the menu, pick something that you always enjoy eating out (such as a gourmet soup). Then order a substantial appetizer for your second course. Finish with a cup of hot decaf, which will get your digestive juices flowing and make you feel cozy and content. This pleasant experience will cost you less than half the price of a "real" dinner out.
- *Become a regular at your favorite restaurant.* It's much better to eat only an appetizer at a good restaurant that you really enjoy than to eat a big meal at an ordinary eatery. It is better for your soul and your health. For business lunches especially, identify the best place in town and

become a regular customer. Learn the owner's name. Become friendly with the staff. You'll be treated like a VIP even if all you ever order is the chopped salad.

- *Order cheap wine in a good restaurant.* Ever since I first became interested in wine, I've had a personal policy about ordering wine in good restaurants: I order the cheapest one of the variety I want. My reasoning is that a good restaurant would never serve a bad wine. Therefore, the cheapest bottle—and almost any restaurant will carry at least one bottle priced at $19 or below—will be good.

  This idea was confirmed by advice I came across in a book titled *The Cheapskate's Guide to Wine* (Kensington, 2001), by Anna Maria Knapp and Vernon A. Jacobs. Their advice is to select a less expensive wine if your entreé costs more than $20 and a higher-priced wine if the entrée is less than $20. The reasoning behind this is that cheaper restaurants recognize that they can't price expensive wines that much over retail and still sell them, so higher-end wines, particularly older vintages, often sell at close to retail prices.

DRINKING LIKE A BILLIONAIRE

The very rich certainly know how to enjoy the finest things in life. This includes wine, champagne, and other alcoholic beverages.

To feel like a billionaire, it's not enough to drink good wine. You have to own it. So get yourself your own little wine "cellar." Even if you have to tuck it away in a closet. If you can, have it refrigerated. (The recommended temperature for long-term wine storage is 58 degrees.)

Drink wine every time you have a sit-down dinner. If that is seven times a week, drink wine seven times a week. Make it a practice to go to your wine cellar and select the wine before the meal is served.

Carefully consider the possibilities. Red? White? Chardonnay? Bordeaux? Consider the menu, your appetite, and what you've sampled in the past. Take your time, and enjoy reading the labels.

When you've finally made your choice, congratulate yourself. You'll have made a major contribution to the dinner—equal to the hour and a half that was spent preparing the food. Return to the table. Pull the cork. Let the wine breathe. When it comes time to pour, tell your dinner guests what they are drinking and why it has been selected. Expect gratitude, even praise. If you don't get any, forgive them. They can't possibly understand what they are getting. Unlike you, they do not know how to live rich.

Before you begin collecting wine for your cellar, there are some important things you need to know. For instance:

- *How to taste wine.* The best way to taste wine is to do everything possible to bring out its full flavor. The way to do that is to swirl it in a good-sized wineglass. Swirling wine exposes it to more air, which allows your nose to pick up more of its aroma.

    When sipping wine, keep your mouth open slightly and draw in a bit of air as you let the wine wash over your palate. You'll be amazed at how much more taste you'll get from it. (This technique makes a slightly unpleasant "slurping" noise, so do it as quietly as possible and only when you mean to really savor the wine.)
- *The right temperature for wine.* You have probably heard a good deal about the "right" temperature for wines. This

subject can seem complicated, but shouldn't be. The general rule is this: White wines should be served chilled, red wines at room temperature. There is a third category—cellar temperature—which means "somewhat chilled." That's the recommended temperature if you're going to store wines for the long haul. The most-often-recommended temperature for this is 58 degrees, which comes closest to the temperature of those cold stone cellars in Bordeaux.

I keep my wine at 58 and can report that it is a good temperature for all wines, but it's especially good for red wines that are just so-so in quality (most Beaujolais would fit into this category) and the lighter whites. The reason I say that is because of the effect temperature has on wines. The warmer the temperature, the more taste is produced. The colder, the less taste. So if you want to ratchet down the taste of a mediocre red, you can chill it a bit (but no more than to about 58). And if you want to bring out more of the taste in a white wine, you can warm it up a bit. (Again, however, you probably don't want to make it warmer than cellar temperature; if you do, it won't feel as refreshing as it should.)

- *Should you smell the cork?* You see this done from time to time. It is not necessary. It may be pretentious. When the waiter puts the cork on the table in front of you for your inspection, you can glance at it to make sure the wine hasn't soaked its way through the entire length—but you don't need to pick it up and sniff it. The purpose of doing this is to tell whether the wine might be soured, and to know *that* you need only taste it.
- *How to learn more about wine. Wine Spectator,* the best-known wine publication in the world, has an online

school with several courses on wine appreciation that you might be interested in. One I might take is on California cabernet, the first of a series of short courses focused specifically on regions. It costs $49. You'll learn the different styles of cabernets, wine geography, how to pair cabs with good cheeses, and price and value comparisons. The course includes video clips of cabernet winemakers, worksheets and study guides, and an online professor to answer e-mail questions. For more information, go to www.winespectatorschool.com.

- *Pairing wine and cheese.* Studies show that eating cheese makes it nearly impossible to taste wine with any discrimination. I'm sure this is true, and yet I've convinced myself that I can tell the difference. If you want to drink your wine and eat cheese at the same time, here are a few generally accepted guidelines:

1. Stilton with port and goat cheese with sauvignon blanc are two classic combinations.
2. Wines and cheeses from the same region usually complement each other.
3. The strength of the wine should be roughly equivalent to the strength of the cheese.

A chart on the *Wine Spectator* web site (www.winespectator.com) lists many more recommendations. Here are some that I think it would be interesting to try:

Barolo and Barbaresco with Parmigiano–Reggiano
Bordeaux (red) with Pyrenees mountain cheeses
Burgundy (red) with Tomme de Savoie
Cabernet Sauvignon with aged Cheddar
Champagne with Brie, Camembert, or Reblochon

Chianti with Pecorino Toscano

Zinfandel with dry Jack or aged Gouda

- *How to open a bottle of Champagne.* Popping the cork of a Champagne or sparkling wine is festive but totally uncool when you're handling an expensive bottle. Rather than let the wine explode, allow the carbon dioxide to ease its way out. To do that, you need to open the bottle with correct form:

1. Place the bottle against your body.
2. Hold the cork firmly with one hand.
3. Turn the bottle (not the cork) with the other.
4. As the cork begins to rise, press against it. Every so often, you'll get an intractable cork. Ten seconds of warm water on the neck of the bottle will solve that.

When it comes to the bubbly, a sigh is better than a pop.

- *Port.* At least one expert considers port "the world's greatest fortified red wine." Port (from Portugal) was created by the British, according to the wine books. The story is that the British, during one of their many wars with France, looked to Portugal for wine. To make the Portuguese wines stable while shipping, they "fortified" them with brandy. The first English port house, Warre, was opened in 1670 in the Portuguese city of Oporto. (Hint: If the wine is really Portuguese, the bottle will be labeled "Porto." If it says "Port," it's produced elsewhere.)
- *Sherry.* Sherry is Spain's oldest world-class wine, dating back to the 1500s. Like port, it is a fortified wine. Properly speaking, sherry comes only from a small zone

SUCCESS WITHOUT A COLLEGE DEGREE

The idea for Internet Security Systems crystallized in 1991, when Christopher Klaus was still in high school. His fascination with Internet security issues led him to develop programs to detect viruses and security breaches. In 1994, when he was only 20 years old, Klaus dropped out of college to found ISS.

ISS went public in 1998, and Klaus—24 at the time—became a multimillionaire. Although he left college long before graduation, he donated $15 million to his alma mater, Georgia Tech. Klaus explained in the *Sarasota Herald-Tribune* that college was a "springboard" that propelled him toward entrepreneurial success.

While he certainly has a gift for working with computers—one former teacher even called him a "prodigy"—Klaus owes his success to hard work and determination. His persistence and resolve have served him well, landing him such honors as one of *MIT Technology Review*'s top 100 young innovators in 1999, a place on the 1999 *Forbes* Top 100 list, and Ernst & Young's Entrepreneur of the Year award for Internet services. Klaus remains actively involved in ISS, but has broadened his horizons to include more than Internet security. Today, he is breaking into the gaming industry with Kareva, a community for online gaming.

Sources: Rob Wright, "The Young & Restless: Christopher Klaus, Internet Security Systems," *VARBusiness*, November 30, 2000; Jason Hall, "Sarasota High Graduate Gives $15 Million Gift," *Sarasota Herald-Tribune*, March 29, 2000.

around the city of Jerez de la Frontera in the southwestern part of the country. If you see "made in Jerez de la Frontera" on the label, you know that the sherry you are looking at is the real thing. Its name, incidentally, comes from the British mispronunciation of the Spanish city Jerez. It was anglicized to "Gerez," which evolved to "Sherry."

ENTERTAINING YOURSELF LIKE A BILLIONAIRE

With today's audio technology, even a $300 boom box sounds great. Spend a grand. Don't even try to tell me you need to spend more than that. The secret is in the music you select—music that makes you feel like a billionaire.

The great thing about books: The best ones cost no more than the worst ones. Treat yourself richly. Read only what makes you feel richer afterward. The same is true for movies, the theater, and just about any other form of entertainment.

There is only one extravagance you can't buy reasonably: front-row tickets to professional sporting events. I have made the mistake of becoming a Miami Heat fan. If you are smart, you will learn to love college ball.

SETTING UP YOUR BILLION-DOLLAR OFFICE

Warren Buffett, one of the world's richest (and smartest) men, keeps his office in a simple building. His walls are paneled in plywood. His desk is a tabletop. He doesn't need the prestige of a cathedral-sized room and an altar-sized desk. He is not God. And he knows it.

But what he does have is a room that is uniquely his, with a comfortable chair and a place for everything he needs. On the surfaces and hanging from the walls are souvenirs to inspire him. Warren Buffett's office is his own. It looks like no one else's office, and it works for him.

That's what you want in your office: the right amount of space, good lighting, a very good chair, and toys that stimulate and inspire you. Everything else is a distraction. And anything that is there simply to make you seem important will only turn off your guests and visitors.

I'm not saying your office should not be luxurious. I am saying it should be luxurious in a personal way. You will be spending most of your waking life in your office, so put as much thought and care into it as you do your home.

If you fill your life with all the best luxuries . . . a great home, great clothes, and delicious food . . . but are too busy running around to enjoy them, you've missed the boat.

Early in this chapter, we talked about the importance of achieving balance in your life—of slowing down and savoring the moment . . . without letting that interfere with your ultimate goal of financial independence. So make sure you never get so caught up in wealth building that you don't take the time to spend at least a half hour a day doing nothing but luxuriating in the rich life that you so richly deserve.

For some people, this is easy. For others, it's tough. If it's hard for you to justify doing it, tell yourself you'll work smarter this way.

Do something with your half hour that a billionaire might do. Sip a cup of espresso. Smoke a cigar. Have a cognac. Contemplate how good life is. Thank the gods for your good fortune. Breathe deeply. Smile.

Then . . . get back to work.

IT'S ALL ENTIRELY WITHIN YOUR REACH

The way you dress, the way you eat and drink—and even the home you live in—can be as good as any billionaire's. Spend time shopping. Buy very selectively. Limit your possessions. And take time every day to really appreciate the good things you have. That's all there is to it. (Oh, yes. And don't scrimp on the mattress.)

INDEX

Index

Index